Tourism and Biodiversity

Achieving Common Goals Towards Sustainability

Tourism and Biodiversity – Achieving Common Goals Towards Sustainability
ISBN: 978-92-844-1371-3

The designations employed and the presentation of material in this publication do not imply the expression of any opinions whatsoever on the part of the Secretariat of the World Tourism Organization concerning the legal status of any country, territory, city or area, or of its authorities or concerning the delimitation of its frontiers or boundaries.

World Tourism Organization
Calle Capitán Haya, 42
28020 Madrid, Spain
Tel.: (+34) 915 678 100
Fax: (+34) 915 713 733
Website: www.unwto.org
Email: omt@unwto.org

Table of Contents

Foreword and Acknowledgements .... **v**

1 Introduction... **1**
   1.1   Tourism and Biodiversity.. 1
   1.2   The UN Responses to Biodiversity Challenges 3
   1.3   Global Initiatives on Tourism and Biodiversity................................ 5

2 The Value of Biodiversity for Tourism.. **7**
   2.1   Understanding the Economic Value of Biodiversity for Tourism 9

3 Impacts of Tourism on Biodiversity **11**
   3.1   Negative Impacts 11
   3.2   Positive Impacts.. 13

4 Biodiversity and Sustainable Tourism **17**
   4.1   The *CBD Guidelines on Biodiversity and Tourism Development* 19

5 Role of the Tourism in Protection of Biodiversity............................ **23**
   5.1   2010 and Post-2010 Biodiversity Target....................................... 23
   5.2   The Economics of Ecosystems and Biodiversity (TEEB) Study................................... 27
   5.3   Implementing the Solutions Proposed by the TEEB....................... 33

6 The Links between Tourism, Poverty Alleviation and Biodiversity **37**

**7 Recommendations for Actions on Biodiversity and Tourism by Governments,
International Organisations, the Tourism Private Sector and NGOs**.......................... **45**

8 Conclusion **51**

List of Tables, Boxes and Figures.. **53**

Annexes
   Annex 1   Typology of ecosystem services 55
   Annex 2   Impacts of Tourism on the Environment and Biodiversity 57
   Annex 3   The 12 Aims for Sustainable Tourism.. 59
   Annex 4   ST-EP Projects Associated with Biodiversity-based Tourism........... 61
   Annex 5   ST-EP Mechanisms and Principles for Pursuing
                  Poverty Alleviation Through Tourism 63

Further Reading... **65**

© 2010 World Tourism Organization – ISBN 978-92-844-1371-3

Foreword and Acknowledgements

This publication looks at the relationship between tourism and biodiversity, and assesses the way that tourism can contribute to the protection of biodiversity and enhance its role as a main resource for tourism destinations. It has been prepared in the context of the International Year of Biodiversity and particularly in preparation for World Tourism Day 2010 and the Tenth Conference of the Parties to the Convention on Biological Diversity (CBD).

The publication will also support UNWTO's activities on tourism and biodiversity in relation to the Rio+20 process, which focuses on a green economy in the context of sustainable development and poverty eradication and other related initiatives such as climate change and tourism, green economy, tourism and protected areas.

The research and writing has been undertaken for the UNWTO by Richard Tapper of the Environment Business & Development Group. Thanks are due to the staff of UNWTO, in particular to Sofía Gutiérrez, Programme Officer, for the concept, supervision and final editing of the paper and to Luigi Cabrini, Director, both of the Sustainable Development of Tourism Programme, for his overall coordination and review; to Marcel Leijzer, Deputy Chief Technical Cooperation and Services Programme; and to the UNWTO Consulting Unit on Tourism and Biodiversity for its timely comments. Special thanks are due to Oliver Hillel, from the Secretariat of the Convention on Biological Diversity for his helpful feedback and comments.

All photographs included in this publication are from participants in the UNWTO Photo Competition 2010, Tourism and Biodiversity, as part of the World Tourism Day celebrations. The cover photo was taken by Tripti Pandey.

Chapter 1 ——

Introduction

1.1 Tourism and Biodiversity

Biodiversity is vital for tourism. Coasts, mountains, rivers and forests are major attractions for tourists around the world. Tourism in the Caribbean, Mediterranean and much of Southeast Asia depends strongly on the recreational opportunities provided by their coastal environments. In southern and eastern Africa, tourism based on wildlife safaris is a dominant attraction and source of income for the tourism sector. Wildlife and landscapes are important attractions for tourism in mountain areas.

Biodiversity plays different roles in different types of tourism. All tourism – even in city centres – relies on natural resources for supplies of food, clean water and other 'ecosystem services' that ultimately depend on biodiversity. For most other types of tourism, biodiversity contributes significantly to the attractiveness and quality of destinations, and therefore to their competitiveness: for example, coastal water quality and natural vegetation are both ecosystem services that contribute to destination attractiveness. And biodiversity is a direct attraction at the heart of nature-based tourism products – such as wildlife watching, scuba diving or tourism in protected areas.

However, biodiversity is under pressure worldwide and has suffered severe losses as more land is converted for human use from a natural state, and as these human uses become more intensive. In 2005, the UN's Millennium Ecosystem Assessment concluded that human activities threatened the Earth's ability to sustain future generations.

Clearance of land for tourism developments has contributed to these losses, particularly in coastal and mountain areas. Inappropriately sited developments have damaged natural coastal defences, making coastal areas more prone to storm damage; or have damaged mountain vegetation and soils, making them more liable to erosion and increasing flooding risks. The physical pressure from the many visitors who are interested in and want to visit sites with rich biodiversity but fragile environments, has also created problems. For example, coral reefs are easily damaged at heavily used scuba diving sites, and the effects of trampling by visitors can change and, eventually, destroy vegetation in mountain areas.

According to current estimates, 60% of the world's land surface is now managed in some way for human use.[1] The loss of biodiversity that has accompanied this intensification of human use of the environment, is measured in the loss of key ecosystems, such as forests, wetlands or coral reefs, and in the growing number of species that are threatened with extinction or which have already become extinct. The rate of species extinction today is reported to be up to 1,000 times greater than the natural rate and ecosystems are functioning less effectively.[2]

Loss of biodiversity is now recognised as a major problem internationally. Healthy ecosystems carry out vital functions – termed 'ecosystem services' – that support life on Earth (box 1). Loss of these ecosystems and of the species they contain, destroys their support functions. For example, natural forests and vegetation act as natural stores of water in watersheds. Destroying these forests leads to increased risk of flooding, erosion and drought as the natural water storage function they perform is lost. Or in the oceans, overfishing in many areas has caused serious declines in fish stocks and has reduced their ability to provide food.

Box 1 Ecosystem services

Healthy ecosystems provide us with ecosystem services. The Economics of Ecosystems and Biodiversity (TEEB) defines ecosystem services as "the direct and indirect contributions of ecosystems to human well-being", and divides them into four main categories:

- Provisioning services – these include supplying food, freshwater and raw materials, such as fiber, timber and fuel wood.

- Regulating services – these include maintenance of soil fertility, pollination of crops by insects, regulation of water flow, prevention of erosion and climate control.

- Habitat services – these maintain genetic diversity amongst species and support species life-cycles.

- Cultural services – these are non-material benefits that include recreation and tourism, education and spiritual experiences.

In addition, these services all depend on supporting services, such as the global water and nutrient cycles, which are fundamental to ecosystem functioning and to life on Earth. These services are vital for tourism; but at the same time, tourism development and activities can adversely affect ecosystems and their ability to provide these services.

The typology of ecosystem services used in the TEEB, along with the supporting services identified in the Millennium Ecosystem Assessment, is shown in annex 1.

In these, and many other examples, biodiversity loss has severe economic consequences due to the costs of the resulting damage: such as a decline in yields from fisheries, or a decline in tourism as a destination becomes less attractive for visitors. Even where there may be technological ways to repair the damage, these are generally far more expensive and less effective than the costs of protecting biodiversity in the first place; and in many cases, technological solutions are either not available or impractical on the scale of response necessary.

Because ecosystem services and biodiversity are vital for tourism, it makes sense for destinations and the tourism sector to protect them as valuable assets that contribute to the long-term success of tourism; furthermore, tourism can provide a positive stimulus for conservation when biodiversity is an important attraction. While this is recognised by many in the tourism sector and in public bodies with responsibilities for tourism, protection of biodiversity and ecosystem services is a shared responsibility that requires coordinated action within the tourism sector and between tourism and other sectors – including government, civil society and NGOs. In particular, this needs to be based on clear frameworks for action, such as national sustainable tourism plans and national biodiversity strategies.

---

1   United Nations Environment Programme (2010), *Are You a Green Leader? Business and Biodiversity: Making the Case for a Lasting Solution*, UNEP, Paris.

2   Ibid.

1.2 The UN Responses to Biodiversity Challenges

The need for action to reverse the decline in biodiversity is recognised in a range of global agreements and initiatives. These include the Convention on Biological Diversity (CBD) and other multilateral environmental agreements, the 2010 Biodiversity Target, the Millennium Ecosystem Assessment (MA), the Millennium Development Goals (MDGs), the UNEP-led study into The Economics of Ecosystems and Biodiversity (TEEB), and the recently established International Science Policy Platform on Biodiversity and Ecosystem Services (IPBES). These agreements and initiatives raise awareness about the issues and provide guidance and frameworks for practical action to protect and restore ecosystem services and biodiversity. In particular, these highlight the importance of measuring and integrating the economic value of biodiversity into policies, planning and decision-making, and of managing biodiversity resources sustainably, so they maintain and enhance ecosystem services. Their guidance and frameworks are as relevant to tourism as to other sectors. The CBD has also produced specific Guidelines on Biodiversity and Tourism Development.

To help reverse the decline in biodiversity, the challenges for the tourism sector and those in government with responsibilities for tourism are:

* applying existing guidance, frameworks and best practices on biodiversity and ecosystems services, to tourism;

* understanding the negative impacts that tourism has on biodiversity and the ways in which these impacts can be avoided or minimised;

* understanding the value of biodiversity for tourism, and the potential for tourism to make a positive contribution to biodiversity conservation; and

* integrating biodiversity considerations into planning and decision-making relating to tourism.

UNWTO has long recognized biodiversity as an important issue. UNWTO and the Secretariat of the Convention on Biological Diversity have been collaborating since the International Year on Ecotourism in 2002. In 2006, UNWTO established the Consulting Unit on Tourism and Biodiversity (box 2). UNWTO will participate in the tenth meeting of the Conference of the Parties (COP 10) to the CBD in Nagoya, Japan in October 2010, to raise awareness of the importance of biodiversity for the sustainable development of tourism. To highlight these links, and to coincide with the UN International Year of Biodiversity, "Tourism and Biodiversity" has been selected as the theme for World Tourism Day 2010.

Box 2 UNWTO Consulting Unit on Tourism and Biodiversity

In 2006, UNWTO, with the support of the Federal Government of Germany established the Consulting Unit on Tourism and Biodiversity for Tsunami Affected Countries, based in the UN premises in Bonn, Germany. The initial goal of this Unit was to provide expertise and advisory support to national and local governments of the countries hit by the tsunami in 2004 (in order to assist in redeveloping their tourist infrastructure). In January 2010, the German Government agreed to continue this cooperation by establishing the UNWTO Unit on Tourism and Biodiversity in a special funding agreement till the end of 2011. The mandate of the Unit has been widened to offer advising services to UNWTO members on issues of tourism and biodiversity upon their request, under the overall guidance and supervision from the UNWTO Secretariat.

The main tasks of the UNWTO Consulting Unit are:

- to provide support to UNWTO Member States on biodiversity-based sustainable tourism, participatory tourism planning, and connecting biodiversity-based tourism to overall economic development;

- to support the development of biodiversity-related sustainable tourism products by local stakeholders;

- to assist UNWTO Member States in finding new funding opportunities for biodiversity-related tourism development projects;

- to highlight the linkages of biodiversity and tourism;

- to raise awareness on the role of biodiversity in adaptation of tourism to climate change;

- to apply the *Guidelines on Biodiversity and Tourism Development* of the Convention on Biological Diversity (CBD) for planning processes in tourism destinations, and demonstrate how this approach can be applied by destinations for management of tourism and biodiversity;

- to develop management, communication and participation tools, as well as training and capacity building for enabling local people to participate in and benefit from tourism projects related to biodiversity;

- to contribute to the formulation and implementation of UNWTO´s activities for the post-2010 biodiversity targets of the Convention on Biological Diversity.

UNWTO is also contributing to the UN inter-agency Environmental Management Group (EMG) report on advancing the biodiversity agenda within the UN system, which also links with preparation of the CBD's Strategic Plan for 2011-2020. The EMG report is contributing to formulation of the post 2010 biodiversity targets and aims to provide information about the interactions of other policy sectors of the UN system with biodiversity; to create awareness in the UN system about the CBD process; and to identify how collaboration in the UN system can be furthered in support of the advancement of the biodiversity agenda. The EMG report is being submitted to the United Nations General Assembly at its tenth special session in September 2010, and to the tenth meeting of the Conference of the Parties to the CBD.

In addition, as part of the UN's Green Economy Initiative, UNWTO, jointly with the UN Environment Programme, is producing a chapter and a series of background papers to show how investment in sustainable tourism solutions can contribute to sustainable development and a green economy. UNWTO's "Roadmap for Recovery", which has been developed to guide governments and the tourism sector in responding to the economic crisis, also highlights the role of the green economy and responding effectively to climate change in the future of travel and tourism.

1.3 Global Initiatives on Tourism and Biodiversity

The tourism sector is already acting to reduce impacts on biodiversity and to support conservation. For example, some tourism businesses have set up funds to support conservation projects and others encourage tourists to make voluntary donations to conservation organisations in the areas they visit. Implementation of sustainable tourism practices is helping to reduce pressures on biodiversity, particularly, by reducing waste generation and improving waste handling and management; by promoting more sustainable use of natural resources, for example through sourcing of food in tourism supply chains; and by managing tourism activities to minimise disturbance to plants, animals and their habitats. Tourism businesses can take many simple actions to help protect biodiversity: The Tour Operators' Initiative for Sustainable Tourism Development (TOI) – whose secretariat is hosted by the UNWTO in Madrid, Spain – in association with UNEP, UNESCO and UNWTO, and various NGOs, has produced guidance on managing tourism in sensitive areas, including deserts, mountains, and the marine environment, and IUCN and Accor have collaborated to produce "Biodiversity: My hotel in action", a guide on biodiversity actions for the accommodation sector.

Some tourism businesses are making important contributions by establishing commercial operations that are directly linked to conservation: one example is the large number of commercial game and conservation reserves that have been established for tourism in southern Africa. Some others have developed tourism products that are specifically designed to support conservation, for example, by providing a share of income to specific conservation projects, and by maintaining a flow of tourists, and therefore income, to areas where income from tourism is a vital source of funding for conservation.

Actions on tourism and biodiversity are also being supported by NGOs and international organisations. The United Nations Foundation, Rainforest Alliance, UNEP, and the UNWTO have led a coalition of over 40 organizations to develop the Global Sustainable Tourism Criteria, which includes biodiversity. The Global Sustainable Tourism Council has been set up to support implementation of the criteria. IUCN has developed various guidance materials on tourism and biodiversity, including Guidelines for Tourism in Parks and Protected Areas, published in 2001 in association with UNEP and UNWTO. UNWTO and the UNESCO World Heritage Centre are jointly working to enhance sustainable tourism management in World Heritage Sites. NGOs including Conservation International, The Nature Conservancy and WWF, and development agencies such as SNV, GTZ, USAID and the World Bank are involved in biodiversity and tourism projects.

Chapter 2

The Value of Biodiversity for Tourism

The value of biodiversity for tourism and the associated services provided by healthy ecosystems is extremely large. The tourism economies of eastern and southern Africa are based on wildlife and outdoor recreation. Around 20% of the land area of South Africa is used for game ranching and conservation, which generate a large proportion of the country's tourism revenues.[1] In Australia, 75% of international and 55% of domestic tourists take part in nature-based or outdoor activities[2] and these tourists generally stay longer and spend more than other tourists. Market surveys have shown that 42% of European travellers, surveyed in 2000, included a visit to natural parks as part of their vacation activities.[3] In England, tourism based on high quality natural environments is estimated to be worth £ 5 billion each year.[4] In the Caribbean, coral reefs generated tourism worth an estimated US$ 4.7 billion in gross and US$ 2.1 billion in net revenue[5] in 2000. In Mexico, Federal protected areas currently receive around 14 million domestic and international tourists, with a total spending of US$ 660 million per year.[6] And in the United States of America, 87.5 million residents participated in wildlife watching, hunting, or fishing during 2006, and spent US$ 122.3 billion on these activities, including US$ 37.5 billion on food, lodging and transportation.[7] 85% of tourism in the United States of America takes place in coastal areas – on beaches, estuaries and wetlands – and far exceeds tourism to theme parks and national monuments.[8] These figures illustrate the scale of biodiversity-based contributions to the tourism economy.

1   Van der Merwe, P. and Saayman, M. (2003), 'Determining the Economic Value of Game Farm Tourism', *Koedoe* 46 (2), pp. 103-112.

2   Tourism Australia (2009), *Activities Factsheet – Year Ending June 2009* (Online), available : http://www.ret.gov.au/tourism/tra/snapshots/sheets/Pages/default.aspx (07-09-2010).

3   Secretariat of the Convention on Biological Diversity (2008), *The Value of Nature: Ecological, Economic, Cultural and Social Benefits of Protected Areas,* Secretariat of the CBD, Montreal.

4   GHK Consulting Ltd. and GFA-Race Partners Ltd. (2004), *Revealing the Value of the Natural Environment in England,* a report to the Department for Environment, Food and Rural Affairs, London.

5   World Resources Institute (2004), *Reefs at Risk in the Caribbean,* WRI, Washington.

6   Secretariat of the Convention on Biological Diversity (2008), *The Value of Nature: Ecological, Economic, Cultural and Social Benefits of Protected Areas,* Secretariat of the CBD, Montreal.

7   US Fish and Wildlife Service (2007), *National Survey of Fishing, Hunting and Wildlife-Associated Recreation 2006,* Washington.

8   Houston, J. R., 'International Tourism and US Beaches', *Shore and Beach* (1996), quoted in *1998 Year of the Ocean – Coastal Tourism and Recreation* (Online), available: http://www.yoto98.noaa.gov/yoto/meeting/tour_rec_316.html

© **2010 World Tourism Organization** – ISBN 978-92-844-1371-3

Of course, tourists who travel to enjoy nature and outdoor recreation engage in other activities as well, perhaps adding shopping trips, concerts, visits to museums, or sports events into their itineraries. Most tourists and other types of traveller, engage in a range of different activities: business travellers may well take tourist excursions, perhaps to a nearby national park, and activities such as scuba diving or whale-watching are commonly offered as excursions in 'sun and sand' tourism resorts. For most tourists, their vacations include multiple activities – and nature-based or outdoor activities that depend on quality environments are a popular option and a frequent motivation for tourists when selecting holiday destinations.

Biodiversity is the major tourism attraction in a number of biodiversity hotspot developing countries, including: Madagascar, Uganda, Tanzania, South Africa, Costa Rica, Ecuador and Belize. Their rich biodiversity is a major factor in the choice of visitors coming to these·destinations, even though only a proportion of them may come primarily to view wildlife. Once in these destinations, visitors may also choose to extend their stays to experience other tourism attractions, such as cultural or heritage sites or recreational resorts. The image created by the biodiversity of these destinations is therefore important for marketing all the forms of tourism they offer, whether or not these are mostly based on biodiversity.

There is significant geographical overlap between tourism development (and growth) and biodiversity hotspots, as well as areas of low human development, as illustrated in a study by UNEP and Conservation International (CI).[9] For example, Argentina, Brazil, Cyprus, the Dominican Republic, India, Indonesia, Macao, Malaysia, Mexico, Morocco, South Africa, Thailand, and Vietnam, each receive over 2 million foreign visitors per year, and have rich-biodiversity. In the North, many major tourism destinations such as the Mediterranean, the California coasts, and the Florida Keys, are also biodiversity hotspots. Even though not all the tourism in biodiversity hotspots is directly based on biodiversity, it is an important factor for a significant amount of tourism in these areas.

The same UNEP-CI study also illustrates pressures that can result from excessive tourism development. For example, foreign visitors outnumber local residents in certain places, while elsewhere the availability of fresh water is already very limited in relation to the scale of tourist arrivals. Although not all the tourism in biodiversity hotspots is directly based on biodiversity, proper planning and effec¬tive management are essential to prevent continued growth of tourism from creating negative social and environmental impacts, including impacts on biodiversity.

9   United Nations Environment Programme and Conservation International (2003), *Tourism and Biodiversity – Mapping Tourism's Global Footprint*, CI, Washington.

2.1 Understanding the Economic Value of Biodiversity for Tourism

From an economic viewpoint, the value of biodiversity for tourism is made up of the price tourists pay for tourism that is based on enjoyment of biodiversity and ecosystem services; their direct and indirect payments to other related businesses for supply of supporting goods and services (such as food supplies, transport, etc.), and to government, through taxes, for provision of infrastructure; and the money that employees in these tourism and related businesses spend in the economy, since their employment, and, therefore, their spending, are dependent on biodiversity-based tourism. It also includes the value that ecosystem services provide to tourism in general, such as freshwater supplies and other provisions, as well as the regulating functions of ecosystems which help protect tourism assets from damage by extreme events, such as flooding or major storms.

In addition, the actual payments made by tourists are often less than they would be willing to pay[10], and this needs to be taken into account in assessing the value of biodiversity for tourism.

While the concepts of the economic value of biodiversity for tourism are straightforward, measuring them is more difficult. In some cases, such as tourism based around coral reefs, the value of biodiversity for tourism has been quantified. But in many cases, it is difficult to quantify this value due to lack of suitable data, limited knowledge about the precise relationship between certain types of biodiversity and tourism, and the multiple uses associated with biodiversity which often make it difficult to define how to split the value of biodiversity between tourism and other uses (box 3).

Information on international travel arrivals is available for most countries, but this does not adequately identify whether each arrival is travelling for recreational tourism, or for other primary reasons such as business or to visit friends and relatives. As previously noted, visitors may engage in some biodiversity-based tourism activities at some stage of their trip, even though this may not be their primary purpose for travel. Information on levels of domestic tourism, the travel motivations of domestic and international tourists, the places they visit and their expenditure can be obtained through visitor surveys, but comprehensive surveys are not available in most cases, or are carried out for marketing and commercial reasons and not published. Furthermore, it is often difficult to combine information from several different sources into a complete picture of the value of biodiversity for tourism, because of differences in the way surveys are conducted and the questions asked.

For these reasons it can be difficult to estimate the value of the contributions that biodiversity makes to tourism: this is not surprising given the limitations of techniques to value ecosystem services, and gaps in knowledge about the linkages between economics and ecosystem dynamics, that are highlighted by

---

10   In economics, this is called the "consumer surplus" and represents the benefit that consumers gain from being able to buy goods and services at lower prices than they are willing to pay.

the TEEB,[11] and which lead ecosystem services to be undervalued or even ignored in decision-making at all levels in both public and private sectors.

> ### Box 3 Multiple uses of biodiversity
>
> In assessing the value of biodiversity for tourism, it is important to recognise that ecosystem services support multiple economic and livelihood activities, and that the value for tourism is therefore only a part of the total economic value of biodiversity. For example, coral reefs support fisheries as well as tourism, and protect the shoreline from damage by extreme events. The value of coral reefs for tourism is just part of the total economic value of reefs. Just as tourism can impact on the value of reefs for other economic and livelihood activities, those activities can also affect tourism. The challenge is to achieve a balance between different economic uses of reefs, and other sources of ecosystem services, that ensures that the overall uses made of these services are sustainable. One example of this is the creation of fish sanctuaries which can be used for tourism activities, such as scuba diving and snorkelling, but where fishing is prohibited. These sanctuaries – such as the Soufriere Marine Management Area in St. Lucia[12] – generate income from tourism, and also protect fish stocks and increase the value of fishing in adjacent areas. Community conservancies in parts of Africa are another example, where communities work together with tourism businesses to decide how to integrate tourism on the land they own, alongside agriculture, hunting and other activities of importance for their livelihoods.

---

11   The Economics of Ecosystems and Biodiversity (TEEB) study is a major international initiative, led by UNEP, to draw attention to the global economic benefits of biodiversity, to highlight the growing costs of biodiversity loss and ecosystem degradation, and to draw together expertise from the fields of science, economics and policy to enable practical actions moving forward. Further information about the TEEB is available at http://teebweb.org/

12   (Online), available: http://www.smma.org.lc/

Chapter 3

Impacts of Tourism on Biodiversity

Tourism has positive and negative impacts for biodiversity. It can be a way of protecting areas from other more detrimental forms of development and of providing an economic basis for investments in conservation and ecosystem restoration, and for generating local employment in areas where there are few other employment options: the value of national parks for tourism and the development of private game parks in South Africa are examples. Tourism also has serious negative effects on the environment arising from land conversion for tourism, inappropriate siting of tourism, pollution and wastes, overexploitation of natural resources, and disturbance of wildlife. It can also create negative social impacts linked to conflicts over resource use, clashes between tourists and local cultural norms and values, or associated with working conditions and opportunities for local people to work in tourism businesses. The main impacts are summarised below, and the full range is listed in annex 2.

3.1 Negative Impacts

The main negative impacts of tourism on biodiversity include the following:

Land conversion for tourism

As tourism continues to expand, more land is converted to tourism uses – for example to provide more accommodation and tourism facilities, such as golf courses or other facilities – and existing tourism areas are used more intensively. The average rate of expansion of international tourism is 3-4% per year globally, although in many developing countries the rate of expansion is at least twice this. Domestic tourism is likely to be expanding at similar, or possibly, faster rates.

Conversion of land to tourism uses results in loss of the biodiversity that it otherwise supports and may also affect biodiversity in surrounding areas, for example a development may prevent free movement of animals thus fragmenting animal populations into smaller groups. Out of nearly 48,000 species of plants and animals included on the IUCN Red List of Threatened Species, 1,761 are reported to be threatened by tourism developments[1]. In addition, much of the world's tourism is concentrated in areas that contain a high proportion of sensitive ecosystems, particularly coastal or mountain regions. These have already been extensively developed for tourism in Europe and North America, and tourism infrastructure is expanding rapidly in many other regions, such as the Riviera Maya in Mexico, Punta Cana in the Dominican Republic, along Turkey's coastline, and in many parts of south-east Asia and China.

Climate change

Tourism contributes to human-induced climate change and to the effects that climate change is having on the distribution of biodiversity as a consequence of changes in rainfall patterns, water availability, temperature and related factors. The tourism sector accounts for around 5% of global carbon dioxide emissions into the atmosphere.[2] These emissions come mainly from air and ground transport, which

---

1   The International Union for Conservation of Nature (2010), *The IUCN Red List of Threatened Species*, version 2010.1 (Online), available: http://www.iucnredlist.org (21-06-2010).

2   World Tourism Organization and the United Nations Environment Programme (2008), *Climate Change and Tourism – Responding to Global Challenges*, UNWTO, Madrid.

make up just over 70% of emissions from global tourism, followed by emissions from accommodation for tourism at 21%.

There is also a risk that adaptation of the tourism sector to the effects of climate change could increase pressures on biodiversity as patterns of tourism change – including expansion into new areas. At the same time, targeted management of biodiversity, such as protection or restoration of coral reefs, coastal ecosystems, wetlands and montane forests, can also assist adaptation and resilience of existing tourism to climate change.

Reduction of carbon emissions remains a priority in the tourism sector, both by using energy more efficiently and by increasing the use of renewable sources of energy, for example as promoted by the Hotel Energy Solutions project[3]. Alongside this, there is also scope for use of voluntary biodiversity-friendly carbon offset mechanisms with accredited verification procedures for carbon emissions reductions achieved through these mechanisms.

Overexploitation of natural resources for food, materials, freshwater and recreation

When resources are used at rates faster than they can be replenished by natural cycles of reproduction or replenishment, they are overexploited. One example of this is global fish stocks, where most of the world's major fisheries have been damaged by overfishing. The tourism sector has a high demand for natural resources, including for foods (particularly seafoods) and materials that are perceived as luxury or prestige items; for large amounts of freshwater in hotels, sports grounds and landscaped areas; and for access to natural areas for recreation.

Planning and development control are critically important for preventing overexploitation of natural resources. In addition, simple operational measures are available to help existing tourism businesses to reduce the pressures they place on natural resources.

Introduction of invasive alien species

Invasive alien species act as vigorous weeds and pests when introduced into areas outside of their natural range. The resulting damage can clog waterways, destroy local ecosystems and damage economically important resources. For example, predation of corals by the invasive crown of thorns starfish (Acanthaster planci) can cause severe damage to reefs, adversely affecting their attraction for tourism, as well as the productivity of the fisheries they support and the other environmental services they provide.[4] The tourism sector itself could also be a source of introduction of invasive species, for instance, through the use of certain attractive but invasive species, such as water hyacinth, in gardens and landscaped areas. The Conference of the Parties to the CBD has noted the issue of tourism as a pathway for introduction and spread of invasive alien species, and has called on the UNWTO and other agencies to raise awareness, and to develop codes of practice and other measures to address this in relation to the tourism sector.[5]

Pollution

Pollution from wastewater, including sewage effluents, and solid wastes produced by tourism, and by use of fertilisers and pesticides on tourism facilities, such as sports grounds and landscape areas, can have adverse impacts on biodiversity. In many parts of the world, treatment of wastewater is minimal, and its disposal leads to eutrophication, a process in which nutrient enrichment stimulates the rapid

---

3   www.hotelenergysolutions.net - Hotel Energy Solutions is a European Commission cofunded initiative: UNWTO is coordinating the project, with the United Nations Environment Programme, the International Hotel and Restaurant Association, the European Renewable Energy Council and the French Environment and Energy Management Agency.

4   IUCN Invasive Species Specialist Group, (Online), available: http://www.issg.org/

5   COP 8 Decision VIII/27 – Alien species that threaten ecosystems, habitats or species (Article 8 (h)); and COP 9 Decision IX/4 – In-depth review of ongoing work on alien species that threaten ecosystems, habitats or species.

growth of some organisms and disrupts healthy functioning of ecosystems. Aquatic environments are very sensitive to eutrophication, and in particular, corals are adversely affected by slight increases in concentrations of nitrogen and phosphorus in the surrounding water.

Solid waste management is also poor in many tourism destinations, and wastes enter the wider environment where they damage wildlife. Use of fertilisers on sports grounds and landscaped areas can also adversely affect water quality in water catchments, and along with pesticides can damage natural vegetation and wildlife.

Disturbance of wildlife

Many animal and plant species are sensitive to disturbance by human activities. For example, vegetation in mountains or coastal dune systems is damaged by trampling and can be destroyed entirely in heavily visited sites, opening them up to risk of erosion. Animals can be affected by disturbance from tourism in many ways. For example cheetahs are less successful in hunting when there are large numbers of tourists and tourist vehicles around; turtle breeding is affected by lights in hotels situated alongside turtle nesting beaches, which can disorientate hatchlings and prevent them from finding their way to the sea; and corals are subject to accidental damage by scuba divers. Disturbance also reduces the breeding success of most species, although some, such as those species common in urban environments, are less sensitive to disturbance than other species.

The negative impacts of tourism can be reduced by various simple measures, including planning controls to protect key biodiversity sites and sensitive areas from tourism development, use of environmental management practices to reduce waste levels and to properly treat and dispose of remaining wastes, implementation of sustainable purchasing schemes to only purchase supplies from sustainable sources, and management of tour groups to minimise disturbance of wildlife.

3.2 Positive Impacts

The main positive impacts include the following:

Employment and economic development

According to the UNWTO, tourism provides more than 75 million direct jobs worldwide.[6] Many of these jobs are linked to the attraction that high quality environments generally have for tourists, in addition to those associated with destinations where nature-based tourism is the main attraction. The income and local employment generated by biodiversity-based tourism can create a strong incentive for communities, local authorities and governments to protect and invest in biodiversity. The examples of game conservancies in Namibia and South Africa demonstrate that tourism linked with conservation is economically beneficial and provides a source of employment.

Export earnings

Tourism is a major source of export earnings in many countries, such as Kenya, South Africa, and many Caribbean States, where the dominant tourism activities are based on biodiversity and high-quality ecosystem services.

---

6   The World Travel and Tourism Council (WTTC) estimate that tourism and travel generates 235 million direct and indirect jobs.

Income for management of protected areas

Revenues from entrance and user fees in protected areas and parks provide funds that can be used for their management. For example, management of Kenya's national parks is mainly funded through tourism, and in fiscal year 2000-2001, Parks Canada generated gross revenues of C$ 84.7 million, including C$ 30.1 million from entry fees, C$ 14.3 million from rentals and concessions, and C$ 10.9 million from camping fees.[7] One estimate suggests that the costs of maintaining a global network of protected areas (estimated at between US$ 1.1 and 2.5 billion per year) represent between 7-15% of the tourism profits generated in destinations that benefit from protected areas as key assets;[8] and that "therefore tourism financial flows have the potential to be a much larger contributor to the management of the world's conservation estate. It has become clear that tourism revenues should not constitute the sole or the most important source of funding for parks (as revenue volume is known to fluctuate with market trends, and as payment for tourism and visitor services is often not linked to biodiversity strategies), but there is a clear growth trend in the contribution of tourism to the funding of protected areas."

Box 4 provides some further examples of income generated through tourism to parks, protected areas and wildlife.

Raising awareness amongst tourists of biodiversity and the need for conservation

The experience of biodiversity and high quality environments can increase the understanding of and support for biodiversity conservation amongst tourists.

Achievement of the positive impacts of tourism requires careful planning, and regular dialogue with local stakeholders during the planning and operation of tourism developments and activities. In particular, tourism will only provide an incentive for biodiversity protection if the income and employment it creates are equitably distributed amongst local residents and communities. If these benefits only go to a few people locally, or if most employees are brought in from other areas, tourism is likely to generate tensions and resentment locally and undermine support for biodiversity protection. It is equally important to ensure that tourism and conservation do not place additional burdens on local people, for example by reducing or preventing their access to livelihood resources. These factors are considered further in the section on tourism, poverty alleviation and biodiversity.

---

7   Secretariat of the Convention on Biological Diversity (2008), *Protected Areas in Today's World: Their Values and Benefits for the Welfare of the Planet, Technical Series No 36,* Secretariat of the CBD, Montreal.

8   Ibid. The estimate is made as follows: "Global international tourism revenues, according to United Nations World Tourism Organization (UNWTO), reached US$ 735 billion in 2006. Based on the conservative assumption that domestic tourism volumes are up to 7 times higher in visitors, with 50% smaller expenditure per head and a resulting 3.5 multipliers, it can be argued that global tourism revenues are in the order of 2,400 billion US$/year. Further assuming that tourism as a business reaches an approximate profitability of 5%, and (again conservatively) that only 15% of global tourism goes to destinations with protected areas, the PA shortfall of US$ 1.7 billion can be estimated to be less than 10% of tourism profits generated in destinations benefiting from protected areas as key assets."

Box 4 Some examples of the value of parks, protected areas and wildlife for tourism

Urban Parks, United States of America

Although cities occupy just 2% of the Earth's surface, their inhabitants use 75% of the planet's natural resources.[9] City parks are valued resources for recreation and urban wildlife. They are also valuable for city economies, increasing property values and municipal revenues, and attracting skilled workers to live and work.[10] An analysis[11] found that spending by visitors who come to the United States cities San Diego and Philadelphia because of their parks, amounted to around US$ 115 million for each city.

Great Barrier Reef Conservation Area, Australia

The total (direct and indirect) value added contribution of tourism to Australia's Great Barrier Reef Conservation Area (GBRCA) in 2006-2007 was A$ 3,344 million, with a further A$ 1,773 contribution elsewhere in Australia from tourists as part of their visits to the GBRCA.[12]

Monteverde Cloud Forest Preserve, Costa Rica

A visitor survey found that 28% of respondents indicated that they would not visit Monteverde Cloud Forest Preserve if the two iconic bird species, the resplendent quetzal and the threewattled bellbird, were missing. This means that US$ 17.5 million out of total tourism income of US$ 62.6 million depends on the protection of Pacific slope habitats of these birds.

Birding Routes, South Africa

The Zululand Birding Route, along with the established Greater Limpopo Birding Route, are worth an estimated ZAR 50 million (US$ 6.8 million) per year in direct economic value to the South African region – most accruing to local people.[13] Birding routes provide tourists with suggested itineraries, trained local guides and birder-friendly accommodation within areas of spectacular avian diversity.

Reintroduction of wolves to the greater Yellowstone area, United States of America

Reintroduction of wolves to the greater Yellowstone area in the mid-1990s has drawn wolf enthusiasts from all over the world to the park. Around 90,000 visitors account for an additional US$ 35 million in spending each year.[14] Local wildlife-watching businesses have adapted to serve the growing demand to view wolves in the wild. They are easiest to observe during the winter months – previously a slow time for tourism businesses and the interest in wolf viewing has enabled these businesses to extend their income-generating season.

Whale-watching in Hawaii, United States of America

The humpback whales' mid-December arrival to their coastal Hawaiian winter feeding grounds dovetails perfectly with the islands' tourist high season, providing local tour operators and other businesses that serve the tourist trade with additional economic opportunities. That translates into more than US$ 11 million in tickets purchased by 370,000 people for humpback whale-

9   United Nations Environment Programme and United Nations Human Settlements Programme (2005), *Ecosystems and Biodiversity: The Role of Cities*, UNEP, UN-HABITAT, Nairobi.

10   'How Cities Use Parks for Economic Development' (2002), *City Parks Forum Briefing Papers 03*, Chicago.

11   'How Much Value Does the City of Philadelphia Receive from its Park and Recreation System? A Report by The Trust for Public Land's Center for City Park Excellence for the Philadelphia Parks Alliance' (2008), Philadelphia and 'Measuring the Economic Value of a City Park System' (2009), The Trust for Public Land, San Francisco.

12   Access Economics Pty Ltd (2008), *Economic Contribution of the GBRMP, 2006-07 Proposal for the Great Barrier Reef Marine Park Authority*, Canberra.

13   BirdLife International Press Release (2008), *Avitourism 'Takes off' in South Africa* (Online), available: http://www.birdlife.org/news/news/2008/04/SA_Birding_Routes.html (09-04-2008).

14   Defenders of Wildlife (2007), *Conservation Pays How Protecting Endangered and Threatened Species Makes Good Business Sense*, Defenders of Wildlife, Washington.

watching excursions each year. In addition, some 62,000 visitors take whale-watching snorkelling trips, adding another US$ 4.5 million each year. The entire whale-watching industry in Hawaii, including viewing the smaller whale species and dolphins, generates in excess of US$ 16 million in boat-excursion ticket sales. Total annual expenditures on other tourist services by some 448,000 whale watchers is estimated at US$ 19 to US$ 27 million.[15]

15   Ibid.

Chapter 4

Biodiversity and Sustainable Tourism

Sustainable development is a driving force in national and international policies for environment and development. It is most commonly defined as "a process that meets the needs of the present without compromising the ability of future generations to meet their own needs".[1] Formally adopted at the UN Conference on Environment and Development, held in Rio de Janeiro in1992, it is now a central principle of international environment agreements, and in the legislation of numerous countries.

Sustainable tourism is tourism that implements the principles and practices of sustainable development. The fundamental objective of sustainable tourism is to make **all** tourism more sustainable. This applies equally to high-volume tourism as well as smaller scale forms of tourism of all types.[2] The relationship between sustainable tourism and biodiversity is simple: sustainable tourism should contribute to conservation of biodiversity.[3]

Since the Rio conference, various sets of principles and criteria have been produced to show how sustainable development can be implemented in the tourism sector. All have a high degree of similarity and following a global initiative led by the United Nations Foundation, Rainforest Alliance, the United Nations Environment Programme (UNEP) and the World Tourism Organization (UNWTO), a set of Global Sustainable Tourism Criteria (GSTC) was launched in 2008. The GSTC were developed through an extensive process of analysis and consultation, taking existing principles and criteria into account. The GSTC provide a set of voluntary standards representing the minimum that any tourism business and/ or certification scheme should aspire to reach in order to protect and sustain the world's natural and cultural resources while ensuring tourism meets its potential as a tool for poverty alleviation.[4]

---

1   World Commission on Environment and Development (1987), *Our Common Future*, Oxford.

2   United Nations Environment Programme and World Tourism Organization (2005), *Making Tourism More Sustainable – A Guide for Policy Makers*, UNEP, Paris.

3   Secretariat of the Convention on Biological Diversity (2007), *Managing Tourism and Biodiversity, User's Manual on the CBD Guidelines on Biodiversity and Tourism Development*, Secretariat of the CBD, Montreal, p.12.

4   http://www.sustainabletourismcriteria.org/.

The GSTC are organised around four main themes:

1)   Effective sustainability planning and management;

2)   Maximizing social and economic benefits for the local community;

3)   Enhancing cultural heritage; and

4)   Maximising benefits and reducing negative impacts to the environment.

The latter contains a specific subsection on Conserving biodiversity, ecosystems, and landscapes, with specific considerations aimed at protecting wildlife species, avoiding introduction of invasive species, and ensuring that "the business contributes to the support of biodiversity conservation, including supporting natural protected areas and areas of high biodiversity value". In addition, it contains a list of potential indicators for guiding biodiversity conservation.

The GSTC provide basic guidelines for tourism businesses of all sizes to become more sustainable, and to help destinations, governments and other stakeholders to formulate programmes for sustainable tourism. The GSTC are consistent with the UNWTO definition of sustainable tourism as tourism that should:

1)   make optimal use of environmental resources that constitute a key element in tourism development, maintaining essential ecological processes and helping to conserve natural resources and biodiversity;

2)   respect the socio-cultural authenticity of host communities, conserve their built and living cultural heritage and traditional values, and contribute to inter-cultural understanding and tolerance;

3)   ensure viable, long-term economic operations, providing socio-economic benefits to all stakeholders that are fairly distributed, including stable employment and income-earning opportunities and social services to host communities, and contributing to poverty alleviation;

4)   sustainable tourism development requires the informed participation of all relevant stakeholders, as well as strong political leadership to ensure wide participation and consensus building. Achieving sustainable tourism is a continuous process and it requires constant monitoring of impacts, introducing the necessary preventive and/or corrective measures whenever necessary;

5)   sustainable tourism should also maintain a high level of tourist satisfaction and ensure a meaningful experience to the tourists, raising their awareness about sustainability issues and promoting sustainable tourism practices amongst them.

The 12 aims for sustainable tourism – elaborated in *Making Tourism More Sustainable* by UNWTO and UNEP to help governments and policy makers with implementation of sustainable tourism – are listed in full in annex 3.

Making Tourism More Sustainable identifies key policy areas which are directly linked to biodiversity and ecosystem services:

Physical integrity

•   Ensuring that new tourism development is appropriate to local environmental conditions.

•   Minimizing the physical impact of tourist activity.

•   Maintaining high quality rural and urban landscapes as a tourism resource.

Biological diversity

- Working with national parks and other protected areas.

- Promoting development and management of ecotourism.

- Using tourism to encourage landholders to practice sustainable land management.

- Working with private parks and reserves.

- Minimizing damage to natural heritage from tourism.

- Raising visitor awareness of biodiversity.

- Raising support for conservation from visitors and enterprises.

Resource efficiency

- Taking account of resource supply in the planning of tourism development, and vice versa.

- Minimizing water consumption by the tourism sector.

- Ensuring the efficient use of land and raw materials in tourism development.

- Promoting a reduce, reuse, recycle mentality.

Environmental purity

- Promoting the use of more sustainable transport.

- Reducing the use of environmentally damaging chemicals.

- Avoiding the discharge of sewage to marine and river environments.

- Minimizing waste and disposing of it with care.

- Influencing the development of new tourism facilities.

In addition, achievement of many of the other aims for sustainable tourism is at least partly dependent on protection of biodiversity. For example, biodiversity plays an important role in visitor fulfilment and community wellbeing; and all aspects of tourism depend on ecosystem services.

4.1 The *CBD Guidelines on Biodiversity and Tourism Development*

The aims and processes of sustainable tourism set out in *Making Tourism More Sustainable* are consistent with the approach of the *CBD Guidelines on Biodiversity and Tourism Development* (box 5). The guidelines and the supporting *Users' Manual,* emphasise the need for tourism to operate in accordance with the principles of conservation and sustainable use of biodiversity. They cover all forms of tourism activity, and are applicable for tourism which has impacts on biodiversity in all geographical locations and tourist destinations.

Box 5 Development of the *CBD Guidelines on Biodiversity and Tourism Development*

The *CBD Guidelines on Biodiversity and Tourism Development,* to which UNWTO contributed, were adopted in 2004, and are consistent with, and contribute to the implementation of international instruments designed to promote sustainability in various areas of tourism, including the 2002 Quebec Declaration on Ecotourism, the 2002 UNEP Principles for Implementation of Sustainable Tourism, the 1999 Global Code of Ethics for Tourism adopted by the World Tourism Organization, the 1997 Manila Declaration on the Social Impact of Tourism, and the 1997 Berlin Declaration on Biodiversity and Tourism. The Guidelines also take into consideration the provisions of the CBD such as the ecosystem approach and the Akwé: Kon Voluntary Guidelines concerning developments that affect indigenous and local communities.

The *CBD Guidelines on Biodiversity and Tourism Development* set out a framework for achieving more sustainable tourism development, by making tourism and biodiversity more mutually supportive, engaging the private sector and local and indigenous communities, and promoting infrastructure and land-use planning based on the principles of conservation and sustainable use of biodiversity.[5] The Guidelines include a process for policy-making, development planning and management to implement this framework. This includes assembling baseline information to enable impact assessment and informed decision-making; formulation of an overall vision and objectives for tourism development and biodiversity management taking local factors into account; impact assessment, management and mitigation, and monitoring and adaptive management. The guidelines stress that multi-stakeholder participation including indigenous and local communities that are or may be affected by tourism development, is central to this process.

Table 1 shows the relationship between the process for implementation of sustainable tourism that is set out in the joint UNEP and UNWTO publication *Making Tourism More Sustainable – A Guide for Policy Makers,* and that of the *CBD Guidelines for Biodiversity and Tourism Development.* Both emphasise that development of clear strategies for sustainable tourism is vital to drive policies and actions, and that this needs to be done through "a participatory process that involves a range of stakeholders in order to foster wider adherence to the strategy and commitment to its implementation." They also highlight the importance of having a market orientation and involving the private sector as stakeholders, for the achievement of sustainable tourism that contributes to biodiversity conservation. In order to succeed, tourism developments (including infrastructure and investments by the public sector, NGOs and communities) need to match the core elements required for commercially-successful development of tourism, including the requirements of tourism businesses and tourists regarding access, security, quality and efficient management.[6]

---

5   Secretariat of the Convention on Biological Diversity (2004), *Guidelines on Biodiversity and Tourism Development,* Secretariat of the CBD, Montreal.

6   United Nations Environment Programme (2005), *Forging Links between Protected Areas and the Tourism Sector. How Tourism Can Benefit Conservation,* UNEP, Paris.

Table 1   Relationship between Processes for Implementation of CBD Guidelines and Sustainable Tourism

CBD Guidelines on Biodiversity and Tourism Development	Making Tourism More Sustainable: A Guide for Policy Makers
Baseline information	Analysing conditions, problems and opportunities
Vision and goals	Identifying objectives and making choices
Objectives	Developing policies and action programmes
Legislation and control measures	The importance of land use planning and development control. Relating tourism strategies to spatial and land use plans. Making land use planning for tourism more sustainable. 'Enabling legislation' in support of tourism sustainability. Reflecting sustainability in national tourism law. Harmonizing and synchronizing legislation. Command and control instruments – enabling governments to exert strict control over certain aspects of development and operation, backed by legislation.
Impact assessment	Environmental Impact Assessment.
Impact management and mitigation Decision-making	The application of specific regulations. Development regulations and planning briefs. Development control processes.
Implementation	Licensing: • Strengthening compliance. • Economic instruments – influencing behaviour and impact through financial means and sending signals via the market. Voluntary instruments – providing frameworks or processes that encourage voluntary adherence of stakeholders to sustainable approaches and practices.
Monitoring and reporting	The use of indicators in policy making and planning. Criteria for selecting and reviewing indicators. Monitoring sustainability.
Adaptive management	Benchmarking. Measurement instruments – used to determine levels of tourism and impact, and to keep abreast of existing or potential changes.
Education, capacity-building and awareness-raising	Capacity building with local communities. Institutional strengthening. Ensuring effective local information delivery and interpretation. Influencing visitor behaviour and awareness.

Chapter 5

Role of the Tourism in Protection of Biodiversity

Planning and development control are critically important for the sustainability of tourism and protection of biodiversity, influencing not only tourism development itself, but also controlling other forms of development that might be detrimental to the economic sustainability of tourism in the short or long term. Protection of biodiversity in relation to tourism requires planning and development of tourism in ways that take biodiversity considerations fully into account and keep the sensitive areas free from development; and operation and management of tourism to prevent or minimize damage to biodiversity, while maximizing the benefits that tourism can bring for biodiversity conservation. This includes measures to ensure that the cumulative effects and scale of tourism do not lead to overexploitation of natural resources in any locality. The mechanisms for this – including use of the planning system, standards and regulation – and are already set out in *Making Tourism More Sustainable* and the CBD Guidelines on Biodiversity and Tourism Development. This section considers the further implications for tourism of the 2010 and post-2010 Biodiversity Target and the solutions developed by the TEEB study.

The tourism sector has both the incentive and capacity to play a significant role in biodiversity protection. As noted earlier, there are many examples of actions by the tourism sector that are helping to protect biodiversity, and to generate economic benefits from biodiversity protection through sustainable tourism. These actions apply to tourism of all types and scales. Even in urban areas, the tourism sector has a footprint on biodiversity over a much wider area: simple actions such as ensuring that food supplies are sourced from sustainable sources, or that hotels promote tours to their guests that benefit biodiversity conservation, can all help to protect biodiversity and ecosystem services.

5.1 2010 and Post-2010 Biodiversity Target

The 2010 Biodiversity Target "to achieve by 2010 a significant reduction of the current rate of biodiversity loss at the global, regional and national level as a contribution to poverty alleviation and to the benefit of all life on Earth", was adopted in 2002 by the Parties to the Convention on Biodiversity.[1] The target

1   In the Strategic Plan for the Convention on Biological Diversity (CBD) **Decision VI/26** of the Conference of the Parties (COP). In **Decision VII/30**, the COP adopted a framework to facilitate the assessment of progress towards achieving the 2010 Biodiversity Target and communication of this assessment, and this was further refined through **Decision VIII/15**.

was endorsed at the UN World Summit on Sustainable Development in 2002, and in 2006, it was fully integrated into the Millennium Development Goals.

The most recent assessment of the status of biodiversity and progress towards the 2010 Biodiversity Target, published in the Global Biodiversity Outlook 3 (GBO3), reports that none of its 11 goals have been achieved, although there has been some progress on some of them, especially in increasing the area of terrestrial ecosystems under conservation.

The overall message of GBO3 is that "we can no longer see the continued loss of biodiversity as an issue separate from the core concerns of society: to tackle poverty, to improve the health, prosperity and security of present and future generations, and to deal with climate change. Each of those objectives is undermined by current trends in the state of our ecosystems, and each will be greatly strengthened if we finally give biodiversity the priority it deserves."

According to the Secretariat of the CBD, for the most part, the underlying causes of biodiversity loss have not been addressed in a meaningful manner nor have actions been directed to ensure we continue to receive the benefits from ecosystem services over the long term. Moreover, actions have rarely matched the scale or the magnitude of the challenges they were attempting to address.

In order to meet the 2010 targets, the GBO3 highlights the need for effective action to address the underlying causes or indirect drivers of biodiversity loss, and in particular for:[2]

* much greater efficiency in the use of land, energy, fresh water and materials to meet growing demand;

* use of market incentives and avoidance of perverse subsidies to minimize unsustainable resource use and wasteful consumption;

* strategic planning in the use of land, inland waters and marine resources to reconcile development with conservation of biodiversity and the maintenance of multiple ecosystem services. While some actions may entail moderate costs or tradeoffs, the gains for biodiversity can be large in comparison;

* ensuring that the benefits arising from use of and access to genetic resources and associated traditional knowledge (for example through the development of drugs and cosmetics) are equitably shared with the countries and cultures from which they are obtained;

* communication, education and awareness raising to ensure that as far as possible, everyone understands the value of biodiversity and what steps they can take to protect it, including through changes in personal consumption and behaviour.

---

2   Secretariat of the Convention on Biological Diversity (2010), *Global Biodiversity Outlook 3*, Secretariat of the CBD, Montreal, pp. 11-12.

The tenth meeting of the Conference of the Parties to the Convention on Biological Diversity to be held in Nagoya, Japan, in October 2010, is expected to adopt a revised and updated set of biodiversity targets for the post-2010 period, as part of the 2011-2020 Strategic Plan for the Convention. A report prepared by the Convention's Secretariat for the Subsidiary Body on Scientific, Technical and Technological Advice has recommended that the Mission of this Strategic Plan is to ensure a coherent implementation of the Convention on Biological Diversity and achievement of its three objectives by promoting "urgent action to halt the loss of biodiversity" and, "by 2020, to: reduce the pressures on biodiversity; prevent extinctions; restore ecosystems; and enhance ecosystem services, while equitably sharing the benefits, thus contributing to human well-being and poverty eradication, and to have provided the means for all Parties to do so." It proposes five strategic goals, that together include 20 targets:

* Address the underlying causes of biodiversity loss by mainstreaming biodiversity across government and society.

* Reduce the direct pressures on biodiversity and promote sustainable use.

* Improve the status of biodiversity by safeguarding ecosystems, species and genetic diversity.

* Enhance the benefits to all from biodiversity and ecosystem services.

* Enhance implementation through participatory planning, knowledge management and capacity building.

In relation to tourism, Governments can make a major contribution to achievement of the post-2010 biodiversity goals by ensuring that there is legislation in place (and enforced), that enables and supports the sustainability of tourism, including protection of biodiversity.[3] In particular, land use planning and development controls can be used to influence the location and type of new and existing tourism activities and to control potentially harmful development. They are critical for the sustainability of tourism, influencing not only tourism development but also controlling other forms of development that might be detrimental to the economic sustainability of tourism in the short or long term. Tourism strategies and biodiversity protection objectives can be integrated into spatial and land use plans considering a wide range of economic, social and environmental factors and based on local consultation and participation. Governments can make land use planning for tourism more sustainable, for example by identifying the nature of and location for new development that will contribute to sustainable tourism; identification of priority areas for the development of tourism that meet sustainability criteria, combined with the use of regulations or development guidelines; and by taking account of already predictable changes in conditions, such as the effects of climate change, introducing adaptation measures and applying the precautionary principle. Use of strategic environmental assessment (SEA), integrated area management,

3   This and the next paragraph are based on the United Nations Environment Programme and World Tourism Organization (2005), *Making Tourism More Sustainable – A Guide for Policy Makers*, UNEP, Paris.

such as Integrated Coastal Zone Management (ICZM), and zoning for tourism development and biodiversity protection are also valuable approaches to land use planning for sustainable tourism and biodiversity conservation.

The role of governments at national and local levels in setting standards and regulations in order to improve sustainability is extremely important in relation to tourism and biodiversity. Examples of relevant standards and regulations include such aspects as the density of buildings, location of buildings (e.g. set-back distances from the coastline), building heights, linkage to services and sewage disposal systems, materials used (e.g. efficiency standards), and aspects of design (e.g. with respect to the local vernacular). Social sustainability issues, such as protection of access to resources of importance for local livelihoods are also relevant to this. Furthermore, planning and controls of tourism activities and development should take into account the cumulative effects of tourism in an area, including resource use and environmental pressures, the density of tourism and the effects that crowding can have on the attractiveness, and hence competitiveness, of a destination.

Tourism businesses can contribute to the post-2010 biodiversity goals by working with governments to ensure that their tourism activities and developments comply with national and local tourism plans and sustainability standards. In addition, tourism businesses can adopt best practices for sustainability in the management of their operations. Guidance on this is available from various sources including UNEP, the TOI and IUCN. Examples of actions that tourism businesses are already taking or can take to help promote and protect biodiversity include:

- ensuring that tourism activities are well-managed and do not damage or disturb wildlife and habitats;

- reducing pollution from tourism activities, particularly by ensuring that all liquid and solid wastes are properly treated and disposed of in ways that do not result in damage to biodiversity, and by minimising use of pesticides, fertilisers and toxic chemicals;

- obtaining all food stuffs, and other biological resources used in tourism activities, from sustainably managed sources;

- working with suppliers and other partners to improve the sustainability of the resources purchased from them;

- creation of wildlife areas and natural habitats in tourism developments;

- establishment of community-based protected areas and co-management systems through which communities lease their biodiversity assets to tourism operations, and which integrate tourism into sustainable land-use management;

- supporting biodiversity conservation by government agencies and NGOs in tourism areas, through practical actions, including financial contributions, for example, through sponsorship and voluntary donations;

- avoiding threatened habitats or sensitive sites when developing tourism activities and facilities;

- ensuring that no invasive alien species are introduced through tourism activities;

- ensuring that no threatened or endangered species are at risk from tourism activities or enter the tourism supply chain (especially as foods or in souvenirs);

- using the communications and marketing strengths of the tourism sector to raise awareness of tourists and destination authorities of the value of biodiversity and the steps they can take to protect it.

5.2 The Economics of Ecosystems and Biodiversity (TEEB) Study

The Economics of Ecosystems and Biodiversity (TEEB) study, led by UNEP, is a major international initiative to draw attention to the global economic benefits of biodiversity, to highlight the growing costs of biodiversity loss and ecosystem degradation, and to draw together expertise from the fields of science, economics and policy to foster sustainable development and better conservation of ecosystems and biodiversity.[4]

The TEEB Study presents the latest ecological and economic knowledge on the value of ecosystem services. Using this, the TEEB has developed guidance for policy makers at international, regional and local levels in order to foster sustainable development and better conservation of ecosystems and biodiversity; information and tools for improved biodiversity-related business practice, particularly in relation to management of risks, business opportunities, and measurement of business impacts on ecosystems and biodiversity. The TEEB also aims to raise public awareness of the contribution of ecosystem services and biodiversity towards human welfare, and of areas where individual action can make a positive difference.

The central message of the TEEB is that while ecosystems and biodiversity provide essential and valuable services that underpin all economic activity, there has been a failure to include the value of these services in economic and other decision-making processes (box 6). This failure to value ecosystem services has led to their overuse and consequent degradation, the extent of which is documented in the Millennium Ecosystem Assessment and the Global Biodiversity Outlook studies.

---

4   The information about TEEB and description of the five TEEB reports, are taken from the TEEB website, http://teebweb.org/.

Box 6 The Economics of Ecosystems and Biodiversity – Key conclusions

"Natural capital – our ecosystems, biodiversity, and natural resources – underpins economies, societies and individual well-being. The values of its myriad benefits are, however, often overlooked or poorly understood. They are rarely taken fully into account through economic signals in markets, or in day-to-day decisions by business and citizens, nor indeed reflected adequately in the accounts of society.

The steady loss of forests, soils, wetlands and coral reefs is closely tied to this economic invisibility. So too are the losses of species and of productive assets like fisheries, driven partly by ignoring values beyond the immediate and private. We are running down our natural capital stock without understanding the value of what we are losing. Missed opportunities to invest in this natural capital contribute to the biodiversity crisis that is becoming more evident and more pressing by the day. The degradation of soils, air, water and biological resources can negatively impact on public health, food security, consumer choice and business opportunities. The rural poor, most dependent on the natural resource base, are often hardest hit.

Under such circumstances, strong public policies are of the utmost importance. These policy solutions need tailoring to be socially equitable, ecologically effective, and economically efficient."

Source: The Economics of Ecosystems and Biodiversity (TEEB) (2009), The Economics of Ecosystems and Biodiversity for National and International Policy Makers – Summary: Responding to the Value of Nature.

To correct the failure to value ecosystem services, the TEEB therefore sets out a framework, and associated methods for assessing the Total Economic Value (TEV) of ecosystem services, using both monetary and non-monetary techniques.[5] The TEEB also recognizes that ecosystems provides bundles of services that are interlinked, and which all need to be taken into account.

Assessment of TEV requires an understanding of ecosystem processes and their relationship to the sustainable delivery of ecosystem services. Sustainable levels of use enable ecosystem services to be provided at a rate that does not exceed the ability of ecosystems to regenerate those services, so that they continue to be available into the future. Put simply, it means adjusting economic methods and decision making to the constraints of natural ecosystem dynamics.

The TEEB defines TEV as a combination of all the immediate ecosystem service benefits, such as freshwater supplies or recreation, and the 'insurance value' that "that lies in the resilience of the ecosystem, which provides flows of ecosystem service benefits with stability over a range of variable environmental conditions". The insurance value is also important in assessing the value of ecosystems in protecting against extreme events, for example, the value of coastal ecosystems in providing storm protection.

The TEEB also highlights the limitations of monetary valuation methods in estimating the value of ecosystem services, since in many instances the information available is not sufficient to allow a full valuation to be made, and since beyond certain thresholds of damage, ecosystems loose their resilience and may undergo irreversible changes. In addition, the values placed on ecosystem services can vary between different groups of stakeholders – for example, a resource may be vital for the livelihoods of local communities, but have much lower importance for national or business stakeholders. Furthermore, the values of cultural ecosystem services may depend on cultural traditions, as well as subjective assessments.

To deal with these issues, the TEEB recommends use of multi-criteria evaluation and deliberative processes, such as citizen juries, or similar mechanisms that enable stakeholders to express independent and informed preferences. The TEEB also recommends that because of uncertainty and existence of ecological thresholds, policy and decision making with impacts on ecosystem services should be guided by the "safe-minimum-standard" and "precautionary approach" principles.

---

5   TEEB – The Economics of Ecosystems and Biodiversity – The Ecological and Economic Foundations, 2010.

The most common methods used for cultural ecosystem services are the travel cost method, which estimates the value of a resource (e.g. a landscape, national park, or a particular species of plant or animal) by measuring the total amount that individuals pay to visit that resource, including their travel, food and accommodation costs; and contingent valuation which uses survey techniques to elicit the willingness to pay for varying levels of environmental services or quality.

In relation to tourism, the TEEB's TEV framework has the following implications:

* The value of tourism is only a part of the TEV of an area.

* Focusing on the value of tourism alone undervalues other important ecosystem services, in turn leading to their overuse and/or depletion, which may also lead to deterioration in the quality of an area for tourism.

* Properly planned and managed tourism can add to the value of other ecosystem services, and can provide an incentive to protect areas from other types of development with more detrimental environmental impacts.

* The tourism sector needs to pay for the ecosystem services it utilises.

* Planning and development of tourism need to take into account the 'insurance value' as well as the immediate benefits of ecosystem services, and ensure that critical ecosystem components are protected from damage or development.

* Local as well as national stakeholders need to be involved in valuing ecosystem services and in decision-making processes concerning plans for and development of tourism.

The TEEB also highlights existing and emerging solutions suitable for wider replication,[6] that include ensuring that payments are made for use of ecosystem services, improving the sustainability of supply chains, using regulation and standards to manage and set limits on use of ecosystem services, and investing in protected areas and ecological infrastructure to expand flows of ecosystem services and increase ecosystem resilience. Table 2 outlines the solutions proposed by the TEEB.

Table 2   Available solutions for better stewardship of natural capital proposed by the TEEB study

Rewarding benefits through payments and markets	Payments for ecosystem services (PES schemes) (e.g. for water provisioning; for REDD-Plus proposals for Reduced Emissions from Deforestation and Degradation, as well as afforestation, reforestation, and effective conservation – if designed and implemented properly). Product certification, green public procurement, standards, labelling and voluntary actions provide additional options for greening the supply chain and reducing impacts on natural capital.
Reforming environmentally harmful subsidies	Global subsidies amount to almost US$ 1 trillion per year for agriculture, fisheries, energy, transport and other sectors combined. Up to a third of these are subsidies supporting the production and consumption of fossil fuels. Reforming subsidies that are inefficient, outdated or harmful makes double sense during a time of economic and ecological crisis.
Addressing losses through regulation and pricing	Many threats to biodiversity and ecosystem services can be tackled through robust regulatory frameworks that establish environmental standards and liability regimes. These are already tried and tested and can perform even better when linked to pricing and compensation mechanisms based on the 'polluter pays' and 'full cost recovery' principles – to alter the status quo which often leaves society to pay the price.

---

6   TEEB – The Economics of Ecosystems and Biodiversity for National and International Policy Makers – Summary: Responding to the Value of Nature 2009.

Adding value through protected areas	The global protected area network covers around 13.9% of the Earth's land surface, 5.9% of territorial seas and only 0.5% of the high seas: nearly a sixth of the world's population depend on protected areas for a significant percentage of their livelihoods. Increasing coverage and funding, including through payment for ecosystem services (PES) schemes, would leverage their potential to maintain biodiversity and expand the flow of ecosystem services for local, national and global benefit.
Investing in ecological infrastructure	This can provide cost-effective opportunities to meet policy objectives, e.g. increased resilience to climate change, reduced risk from natural hazards, improved food and water security as a contribution to poverty alleviation. Up-front investments in maintenance and conservation are almost always cheaper than trying to restore damaged ecosystems. Nevertheless, the social benefits that flow from restoration can be several times higher than the costs.

Source: Based on the Economics of Ecosystems and Biodiversity (TEEB) (2009), The Economics of Ecosystems and Biodiversity for National and International Policy Makers – Summary: Responding to the Value of Nature.

The solutions advocated by the TEEB are all relevant to tourism, and the following sections outline how they could be applied in the tourism sector:

Rewarding benefits through payments and markets

The tourism sector needs to shift to a system where the contribution of ecosystem services to tourism is recognized and paid for, for example through establishment of Payments for Ecosystem Services (PES) schemes; and continue efforts to improve the sustainability of supply chains and reduce their level of use of ecosystem services.

There are already examples of PES schemes in operation in the tourism sector, including entrance and user fees (e.g. dive fees) charged by some protected areas, or carbon offset fees that some tourism businesses have started to introduce on a voluntary basis. At national level, the TEEB shows how governments can also implement PES through tax mechanisms, provided that there is a clear link between that tax and ecosystem services. A key consideration in implementation of PES schemes is the most efficient and effective way in which payments can be collected and linked to protection of the ecosystems that provide the services for which payments are collected. Box 7 illustrates the relationship between economic flows generated by ecosystem services, using protected areas as an example.

Box 7 Tourism and ecosystem services – Economic flows using protected areas as an example of an ecosystem service

A simplified model of the monetary flows associated with tourism and protected areas

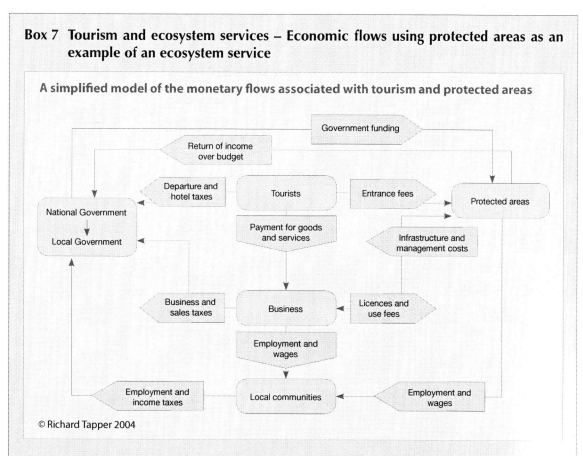

© Richard Tapper 2004

This diagram illustrates the main economic flows associated with tourism in protected areas. Understanding these flows helps to show the ways in which tourism based on the biodiversity of protected areas contributes economically at national and regional levels, as well as at the level of individual sites. The flows also apply to biodiversity-based tourism generally, although entrance and use fees will not apply to areas where there is free public access.

While tourists pay for access and use of protected areas, they also pay for accommodation, transport and other goods and services to enable them to travel to and visit these sites: these payments in turn generate tax revenues and further expenditures within the economy. Increasing the economic benefits of tourism to protected areas requires strengthening of all monetary flows, including by investment in conservation, by development of more biodiversity-based tourism products, and by increasing employment and economic benefits in local communities. Tourism's contribution to conservation of protected areas can be either be generated directly from entrance and use fees (provided these can be retained for conservation) or be provided by government through the tax system from the overall tax revenues generated from biodiversity-based tourism.

Source: Wildlife Watching and Tourism: A study on the benefits and risks of a fast growing tourism activity and its impacts on species, UNEP/CMS Secretariat (2004), Bonn.

The tourism sector has already developed mechanisms for sustainable supply chain management (e.g. The TOI has developed a guide on supply chain engagement for tourism operators; growing numbers of European tourism organisations are adopting the Travelife management systems and tools, which include a supplier tool, to introduce of sustainability principles in tourism).[7] The sector already has a range of certification and labelling linked to sustainability, and the recently formed Global Sustainable Tourism Council (GSTC) is working with the sector to implement the Global Sustainable Tourism Criteria[8] developed through a global initiative led by the United Nations Foundation, Rainforest Alliance, the

---

7   Tour Operators' Initiative (2004), *Supply Chain Engagement for Tour Operators: Three Steps Toward Sustainability,* TOI. See also Travelife Sustainability System (Online), available: http://www.travelife.eu/.

8   www.sustainabiletourismcriteria.org.

United Nations Environment Programme (UNEP) and the World Tourism Organization (UNWTO). The GSTC is developing educational materials and technical tools to guide hotels and tour operators in implementing the criteria.

Reforming environmentally harmful subsidies

Examples of environmentally harmful subsidies include those that keep the price of fossil fuel energy artificially low, contributing to the environmental problems associated with production and consumption of fossil fuels. In relation to tourism, there is a risk that direct or indirect subsidies, including grants, tax breaks or concessional financing, can lead to overdevelopment and unsustainable use of local ecosystem services. At the same time, subsidies can be used to promote investment by tourism businesses to improve their sustainability and reduce pressures on ecosystem services. There is a need to identify and reform environmentally harmful subsidies that may be applied to the tourism sector.

Addressing losses through regulation and pricing

Use of regulations at both national and local level is an important tool for ensuring protection of key ecosystem services. Examples of regulations, that protect ecosystem services and which affect the tourism sector, include establishment of protected areas, controls on development in sensitive locations (e.g. set-back distances from the coastline) and on the overall level of development in a destination (e.g. planning frameworks, zoning), regulations on waste water discharges, water use, etc. Biodiversity and ecosystem services considerations need to be integrated fully into planning and regulatory frameworks for tourism, and where appropriate limits may need to be set on the cumulative extent and type of tourism development, in order to maintain a balance between tourism and protection of biodiversity and ecosystem services, and also to maintain the attractiveness of tourism products and destinations in the long-term. It may also be necessary to strengthen planning and management of tourism particularly at destination-level, so that public authorities are equipped with information and tools (e.g. integrated land-use and landscape planning; Strategic Environmental Assessment (SEA); CBD Guidelines on Biodiversity and Tourism Development; participatory methods for stakeholder consultation) to plan frameworks for tourism development and management for integrating ecosystem services into planning, and to enhance monitoring and enforcement of planning decisions and regulations.

Adding value through protected areas

Tourism can be a significant source of value for protected areas. However, not all protected areas are suitable for tourism activities, either because they are too sensitive to impacts of visitation, or because they are difficult to access, lack suitable local accommodation for tourists, or subject to security concerns.[9]

Tourism that does take place in protected areas needs to be conducted in ways that are compatible with conservation objectives in those areas, and to generate sufficient revenues to cover costs of their protection and conservation, and of management of tourism (including provision of appropriate quality and scale of tourism facilities, rangers/guides, and maintenance). In many cases, protected areas use entrance and user fees to raise revenue from tourism, while some are also able to raise revenue through concessions and commercial activities. In addition, some tourism companies make donations, and/ or encourage their clients to donate to protected areas they visit. While the tourism sector needs to generate sufficient revenues to pay for the ecosystem services that protected areas provide for tourism, protected areas also need to develop and implement effective tourism management plans that integrate tourism alongside their conservation management priorities and establish limits on the scale and

9   United Nations Environment Programme (2005), *Forging Links between Protected Areas and the Tourism Sector. How Tourism Can Benefit Conservation*, UNEP, Paris.

types of tourism permitted, for example, based on the CBD Guidelines on Biodiversity and Tourism Development.

It should be noted that protected areas often are not sufficiently funded to enable effective conservation management, and that where tourism takes place, there may be opportunities to increase funding for protected areas from the tourism sector either directly (via fees and voluntary contributions) or through government funding (based on the contribution of tourism to the national economy, and the tax revenues generated through tourism).

Investing in ecological infrastructure

Investment in ecological infrastructure in relation to tourism includes conservation of sites and areas that provide key ecological services for tourism, ensuring that this infrastructure is protected from damage by tourism developments (e.g. in coastal areas by ensuring proper set-back, protection of coastal features, forests, wetlands, etc.), and investing in existing and new ecological infrastructure (e.g. artificial reefs, no-take fish sanctuaries, mangrove restoration, habitat restoration) which can generate opportunities for tourism.

5.3 Implementing the Solutions Proposed by the TEEB

Implementing the solutions identified by the TEEB will result in better stewardship of ecosystem services and natural capital. The proposed solutions will require changes in decision-making and practices within public and private sector organisations to recognise the value of biodiversity, and the TEEB highlights the importance of collaboration and partnerships for creating these changes at all levels. In particular, the TEEB identifies a need for collaboration between international institutions and the national level to create the necessary policy changes to establish the framework for integrating the value of biodiversity and ecosystem services into planning and decision-making, and the importance of local management within this framework for sustainable use of biodiversity and ecosystem services. It also stresses the need for citizens and NGOs to be actively engaged in these changes, since biodiversity and ecosystem services are generally public goods. The UNWTO can play its role by working with other UN organisations, with Tourism Ministries, National Tourism Boards and Destinations and with the tourism private sector, to establish practical ways to apply the findings of the TEEB to the sustainable management and development of tourism.

Box 8 describes how an integrated planning approach, supported by the UNWTO Consulting Unit of Tourism and Biodiversity, has worked with the participation of all relevant stakeholders to enhance sustainable tourism and biodiversity conservation in Pangandaran, a growing centre of domestic and international tourism in Indonesia. And box 9 describes the benefits of using a coordinated approach to planning and implementation of sustainable tourism components in Mexico, Namibia and Malta.

Box 8 Sustainable tourism and biodiversity conservation in Pangandaran, Indonesia

Pangandaran is a growing centre of tourism for domestic and international tourists on the south coast of Java. Its attractions include beaches that rival those of Bali, and the Pananjung Nature Reserve with a rich fauna that includes wild ox, deer, monkeys and birds. The resort was badly damaged by the Indian Ocean tsunami in 2006.

Weak tourism management in Pangandaran had led to negative impacts on the quality of the environment. In particular, pollution of the sea with garbage and waste-water from the tourism sector, had resulted in a loss of sea water quality and significant damage to the coral reef and marine biodiversity.

In collaboration with the Government of Indonesia, and with support from the Federal Government of Germany, Pangandaran was selected for a demonstration project in the UNWTO Consulting Unit on Tourism and Biodiversity programme "Tourism Development Supporting Biodiversity Conservation". The project's overall goals are to enhance sustainable tourism development in harmony with biodiversity conservation in Pangandaran. The project has developed a detailed tourism planning and management scheme, supported development of tourism products and adequate tourism-related infrastructure, and implemented a range of measures for stakeholder empowerment, communication and cooperation on local, regional and national levels.

The tourism management plan has been developed through an extensive collaborative process that has involved all key stakeholders, working in close cooperation with INDECON (Indonesia Ecotourism Network) and local experts. Based on methods from the *Users' Manual* on the CBD Guidelines for Biodiversity and Tourism Development, this plan establishes defined zones for different types of tourism and land use: it ensures protection for the key environmental services provided by the Pananjung Nature Reserve and coastal ecosystems, and creates additional tourism opportunities such as hiking and bird watching.

Actions taken through the project have improved tourism management and enforcement of regulations in Pangandaran and the Pananjung Nature Reserve, and have raised awareness amongst tourism businesses, local residents and tourists of the importance of protecting natural resources. The zoning of the area, including areas where tourism and development is not allowed, has stopped further loss and damage of habitats, such as the core zone of the Reserve, where damage was threatening populations of wild ox and other mammals.

The project has begun construction of an artificial coral reef, which will benefit local fish stocks as well as providing sites for scuba diving. An "Adopt a Coral" tourist activity has been set up to raise awareness, generate income and involve tourists in the reef construction. Further initiatives includes development of an interpretation trail and guidebook for tourists visiting Pananjung Nature Reserve, and of a series of walking, boating and biking activities linked with village tours.

The project demonstrates the importance of an integrated approach that brings together all relevant stakeholders to address all land-use issues, including uses for tourism and conservation. It has led to greater cooperation between local communities and businesses, including development of new tourism products that generate income for local communities and add to the interest of Pangandaran for tourists, while protecting and managing natural resources in a sustainable way.

Source: UNWTO Consulting Unit on Tourism and Biodiversity.

Box 9 Policy processes for sustainable tourism in Mexico, Namibia and Malta

Strategic Environmental Assessment of Mexican Tourism[10]

Background: Tourism accounts for approximately 9% of Mexico's GDP. It is the country's third largest source of foreign currency (US$ 10.8 billion per year), drawing more than 52 million domestic and 20 million international visitors in 2004. However, if de-linked from sustainable planning and investment, tourism growth can threaten the very resources on which it is based. In a 2002 tourist survey, environmental quality – one of the key determinants for selection of tourist destinations – received the lowest rating. Mexico's 2001-2006 National Development Plan emphasised the need for economic development with human and environmental quality.

Approach: A strategic environmental assessment process of the tourism sector was initiated to formulate and implement a sustainable policy for tourism in the country. To ensure broad participation and commitment across sectors, an Intersectoral Technical Working Group was established, drawing on representatives from the tourism, environment, forests, water and urban development sectors and the interior and finance ministries. It set sector priorities, an action plan for implementation and medium-term monitoring indicators. The group has since been formalised as the Intersectoral Commission for Tourism.

Key benefits: Several benefits were realised from the assessment:

- It provided environmentally-based evidence to support informed decisions. It identified environmental opportunities and constraints associated with different growth scenarios, as well as priorities consistent with optimising the benefits of tourism without overexploiting the environment.

- The approach translated into participation from all sectors and relevant stakeholders. The working group enabled parties with different mandates over natural resources and other issues to make durable commitments and reach agreements with a long-term perspective.

- The findings of the analytical work are informing a policy for sustainable development of tourism.

Financing Namibia's Protected Areas[11]

Background: Studies have highlighted tourism – particularly centred around the nation's wildlife – as one of Namibia's most important industries. Indeed, purchases of services by foreign tourists were estimated to be about 3,100 Namibian dollars (N$) in 2003, accounting for some 24% of the country's total exports of goods and services. Although Namibia's protected area system has significant economic value because of the direct and indirect income it generates through tourism and wildlife industries, its management was heavily dependent on a limited budgetary appropriation that was far from sufficient. Shortages of funds meant that the protected area system struggled to meet its conservation objectives and that there was little investment in it.

Approach: To facilitate more adequate income flows for enhanced protected areas management, the Ministry of Environment and Tourism, with support from the GEF and UNDP, estimated the economic values associated with the protected area system with a view to using this information as a basis for planning investments in the system over the next decades.

Outcome: The study found that the protected areas contribute between N$ 1 billion to N$ 2 billion to the national economy. Demonstrating the economic contribution of Namibia's protected areas led to an increase in core funding from N$ 50 million to N$ 110 million. This increase is in turn expected to generate a positive rate of return of 23%.

---

10   From: World Bank 2005, cited in OECD 2006b, quoted in UNDP-UNEP Poverty-Environment Initiative (2009), *Mainstreaming Poverty-Environment Linkages into Development Planning: A Handbook for Practitioners.*

11   From: Turpie et al. 2004 quoted in UNDP-UNEP Poverty-Environment Initiative (2009) *Mainstreaming Poverty-Environment Linkages into Development Planning: A Handbook for Practitioners.*

The study highlighted the need to understand true costs, economic contribution and potential revenue streams for parks. It also demonstrated that the survival and success of the protected area system increasingly depends on strengthening funding. This includes funding by international grants and government, and by capturing more of the existing and potential direct use value. The study concluded that it was critical to develop incentives – that is, to retain revenues earned within the park agency.

Malta National Carrying Capacity Assessment (CCA) and its application in tourism policy[12]

Malta has a high population density (1.200 inhabitants per km^2), and limited natural resources. The CCA is a tool to identify the optimal level of future development of the Maltese islands. The CCA identified different scenarios of future development (free development scenario, limited growth scenario, low growth scenario, upmarket scenario). It analysed all issues, from resource consumption and transportation to the social acceptability of tourism. Based on considerations of economic dependency on tourism, the present allocation of resources, the social implications and the need to maintain a high level of visitors' satisfaction, the CCA committee favoured the limited growth scenario. A key argument for controlling growth in bed stock was the need to increase the occupancy rate of hotels up to 65%. The CCA resulted in detailed recommendations, in the fields of public transport, land management, water consumption, energy production, waste management, and beach management. The assessment concluded that 160.000 tourists per month is the maximum socially acceptable level of visitation for Malta. The CCA has provided Malta with a powerful tool for sustainable tourism planning.

---

12   Source: Mr. Francis Albani, Director of Tourism and Corporate Services at the Malta Ministry for Tourism and Culture – presentation included in World Tourism Organization (2007), *Policies, Strategies and Tools for the Sustainable Development of Tourism*, UNWTO, Madrid.

Chapter 6

The Links between
Tourism, Poverty Alleviation and Biodiversity

Part of the pressure on biodiversity arises from unsustainable use of natural resources by those in poverty just in order to survive. Therefore reducing poverty should also lead to reduction of pressures on biodiversity, and help to restore uses of natural resources to sustainable levels. In this context, the development and promotion of tourism can serve as a viable way to derive socio-economic benefits from the natural heritage of a destination, creating employment and income generating opportunities for poorer and disadvantaged groups of the society. The local value created by tourism based on biodiversity should provide a further incentive for communities to ensure that their natural resources are used sustainably.

The links between poverty alleviation and biodiversity are widely recognised, for example, in the Millennium Development Goals and the 2010 Biodiversity Target, and are also addressed in the TEEB study. But while progress is being made towards the Millennium Development Goals and the 2010 Biodiversity Target, the rate of progress is far slower than is needed or was planned. This reflects the complexity of poverty alleviation and reducing biodiversity loss, the scale of action needed, and the difficulty of maintaining and translating political will into actions on-the-ground. In particular, to make lasting progress, it is necessary to change policies and institutions so that they provide strong and coordinated frameworks for poverty alleviation and environmental protection – a process termed "poverty-environment mainstreaming".[1]

UNDP and UNEP define poverty-environment mainstreaming as the process of integrating poverty-environment linkages into policymaking, budgeting and implementation processes at national, sector and subnational levels. It is an iterative, multi-year, and multi-stakeholder effort that involves coordination across ministries as well as civil society, academia, business and industry, general public and communities, and the media and development actors.

Figure 1 illustrates the relationship between poverty reduction and environmental preservation. Poor people and communities rely more directly on environmental resources for their livelihoods than other groups. Therefore ensuing protection of those resources is vital for poverty reduction, and long-term poverty reduction requires both poverty reduction measures and measures for environmental protection.

The agenda for sustainable tourism set out in *Making Tourism More Sustainable* and the *Global Code of Ethics for Tourism* (box 10), address these issues, and place particular emphasis on participation of local communities in tourism developments that affect them, from the earliest planning stages onwards.

---

1   UNDP-UNEP Poverty-Environment Initiative (2009), *Mainstreaming Poverty-Environment Linkages into Development Planning: A Handbook for Practitioners.*

Box 10 Extracts from the *Global Code of Ethics for Tourism* addressing sustainable development, environmental protection and benefits for host countries and communities

Article 3 – Tourism, a factor of sustainable Development

[...]

4.   Tourism infrastructure should be designed and tourism activities programmed in such a way as to protect the natural heritage composed of ecosystems and biodiversity and to preserve endangered species of wildlife; the stakeholders in tourism development, and especially professionals, should agree to the imposition of limitations or constraints on their activities when these are exercised in particularly sensitive areas: desert, polar or high mountain regions, coastal areas, tropical forests or wetlands, propitious to the creation of nature reserves or protected areas.

[...]

Article 5 – Tourism, a beneficial activity for host countries and communities

1.   Local populations should be associated with tourism activities and share equitably in the economic, social and cultural benefits they generate, and particularly in the creation of direct and indirect jobs resulting from them.

2.   Tourism policies should be applied in such a way as to help to raise the standard of living of the populations of the regions visited and meet their needs; the planning and architectural approach to and operation of tourism resorts and accommodation should aim to integrate them, to the extent possible, in the local economic and social fabric; where skills are equal, priority should be given to local manpower.

[...]

The links between tourism, poverty alleviation and biodiversity are evident in the ST-EP programme, launched by UNWTO in 2002, with support from The Government of the Republic of Korea, the Netherlands Development Organisation SNV, the Italian Government, the French Government and a wide range of other development agencies and private sector organisations. With this support, 90 STEP projects are already under implementation, benefiting 31 countries in Africa, Asia, Latin America and the Balkans, as well as 3 regional ST-EP projects in West and Southern Africa. The ST-EP projects focus on a wide range of activities, such as training of local guides and hotel employees, facilitating the involvement of local people in tourism development around natural and cultural heritage sites, establishing business linkages between poor producers and tourism enterprises, providing business and financial services to small, medium and community based tourism enterprises, and development and promotion of community based tourism initiatives. Box 11 describes a biodiversity-based tourism project undertaken by the ST-EP programme in Cambodia, and a full list of such projects is provided in annex 4. Details of the ST-EP mechanisms and the principles for poverty alleviation through tourism are shown in annex 5.

In a number of the ST-EP projects, the tourism component is based on biodiversity. Similarly, the UNWTO's Biodiversity Unit projects in Indonesia and Thailand include components from the ST-EP mechanisms and the principles for poverty alleviation through tourism.

The importance of biodiversity in projects that use tourism as part of a mechanism for poverty alleviation reflects the fact that biodiversity is likely to be one of the few assets available to poor communities. It also underlines the need for long-term environmental protection in order to support the long-term success of sustainable tourism. However, existence of biodiversity assets is not on its own sufficient for, first, the successful development of tourism, and second, for successful tourism to be effective in poverty alleviation.

Successful development of tourism in a locality depends on accessibility to major sources of tourists (determined by transport infrastructure, reliability and travel times), availability of suitable accommodation, considerations of health and security, and availability of reliable local businesses supporting tourism.[2] Furthermore, making links between tourist markets at some distance from a locality, and the tourism opportunities that a locality offers, is complex and generally dependent on third party intermediaries, such as travel agencies or tour operators. These intermediaries are vital in providing tourism sites with the necessary market access to generate a flow of tourists; however, in choosing which sites to promote they pay particular attention to other alternative sites that are available, marketability and potential level of demand from tourist. Hence even sites with apparent tourism potential may fail to gain significant market access if there are alternative sites that are preferred by tourism intermediaries. Although in theory sites could seek to develop direct market access, in practice this option is very rarely a financially viable.

Secondly, successful development of tourism does not guarantee that tourism will be effective in poverty alleviation. Poverty alleviation itself is a complex process that involves a combination of macro-level policy measures and programmes and micro- level actions. Poverty is experienced by people who do not have access to sufficient resources or income to meet their basic needs. It is far more than a lack of income: it is characterized by hunger and malnutrition, poor health, lack of access to water and sanitation, lack of participation in education, lack of marketable skills, insecurity and vulnerability.[3] The challenge of poverty alleviation and development is to improve the quality of life and enlarge people's choices; and the measure of success or otherwise of poverty alleviation programmes is the change in the proportion of people whose basic needs are met reliably and consistently taking into account their vulnerability to shocks and trends, such as illness, market volatility or climatic change.

Tourism can contribute to poverty alleviation where it results in more people being able to meet their basic needs. This will generally be through increased local employment or small business opportunities linked to tourism, either directly, or through supply of goods and services to the tourism sector. However creation of jobs and income flows through tourism does not mean that those jobs or income flows will necessarily benefit local people and communities: for example, local people may lack the necessary skills for employment in the tourism sector, or have insufficient assets to be able to develop businesses that can take advantage of the economic activity generated by tourism.

2   United Nations Environment Programme (2005), *Forging Links between Protected Areas and the Tourism Sector. How Tourism Can Benefit Conservation,* UNEP, Paris.

3   World Tourism Organization (2004), *Tourism and Poverty Alleviation – Recommendations for Action,* UNWTO, Madrid.

Figure 1 Examples of poverty-environment linkages

Environmental preservation

Win-Lose	Win-Win
Environmental management that excludes local communities (i.e. lack of benefit-sharing, dislocation of communities)	Sustainable livelihoods (e.g. sustainable agriculture, forestry, fisheries, ecosystem management, adaptation to climate change)
Lose-Lose	**Lose-Win**
Lack of adequate environmental management negatively affecting the poor (e.g. lack of adaptation to climate change, poor environmental health conditions)	Short-term livelihoods (i.e. overgrazing, overfishing, deforestation)

Poverty reduction

Source: UNDP-UNEP Poverty-Environment Initiative (2009), *Mainstreaming Poverty-Environment Linkages into Development Planning: A Handbook for Practitioners.*

However, there are many examples where tourism has led to tensions and conflicts between tourism businesses and local communities, undermining its ability to contribute to poverty alleviation. These conflicts may be over use of resources, particularly land, freshwater or marine resource of importance for local peoples' livelihoods; over the social impacts that tourism can have on local communities, for example, where the dress and behaviour of tourists clashes with local cultural values; or over the extent to which local people are employed in tourism businesses, their remuneration and conditions of work. Tourism developments or activities that result in conflicts of these types with local communities, do not assist in poverty alleviation.

Box 11 ST-EP Project – Cambodia: Mekong Discovery Trail and Tourism Development Master Plan for Kratie Town

In Cambodia, the ST-EP Programme is supporting the development of tourism in the northeastern provinces of Stung Treng and Kratie, focusing on the town of Kratie as a gateway destination and taking advantage of the Mekong River to provide opportunities for eco- and community-based tourism. The project is being implemented in three phases through a collaboration between the Ministry of Tourism of Cambodia, SNV, the ST-EP Foundation and UNWTO, in an effort to bring local economic development to one of the least developed regions in Cambodia.

During Phase One, which was completed in September 2007, the project prepared a Tourism Development Master Plan for the town of Kratie and provided recommendations on a number of actions to be taken by a variety of tourism stakeholders to realize the goal of transforming Kratie into an attractive tourism destination, in order to extend visitor's length of stay and to increase the number of visitors to the area.

Some of these recommendations have been implemented during Phase Two, such as the expansion and diversification of tourism products and activities, by developing the Mekong Discovery Trail to connect Kratie's main tourism attractions with nearby ecotourism activities on the Mekong river islands and shores.

The Mekong Discovery Trail is being designed and developed in close cooperation with the provincial authorities and local communities. The project undertook an analysis of tourism over the proposed 190-km route in Kratie and Stung Treng Provinces, including the identification and evaluation of tourism resources along the trail and assessment of their role for tourism attractions and activities.

During the tourism analysis, the project also identified selected villages along the Mekong River with potential for eco- and community-based tourism development and formulated community preparation plans for these villages. The community preparation plans pay special attention to the detailed design and development of guidelines for each village/community; the development of supporting tourism products, crafts, and commodities; down and up stream economic activities and their application to each community, and development of alternative livelihoods; development of mechanisms for equitable benefit sharing between the stakeholders, and assessment of energy needs and mechanisms to minimize pollution. In its third phase the project is implementing some of these community preparation plans, which include awareness building and guide training for the villagers in the areas of ecotourism, heritage/cultural tourism, and associated skills.

For the overall product development and marketing of the Mekong Discovery Trail, the project undertook initial market demand and supply forecasting to identify the broad and target market segments and to guide development of itineraries for the various trail routes and products. For awareness-raising and promotion, familiarization trips for regional media and travel trade were conducted, and a website for the Mekong Discovery Trail has been developed (www. mekongdiscoverytrail.com).

Source: UNWTO Technical Cooperation and Services Programme.

There are also structural barriers that may limit the ability of poor people and communities to benefit from tourism. These barriers can include:

* lack of sufficient skills or education to be successfully employed in tourism;

* lack of links with intermediaries in the tourism value chain (limiting the ability to successfully market goods and services in the tourism sector);

* lack of sufficient assets to be able to take advantage of potential opportunities from development of tourism;

• lack of secure property rights or land title to those areas providing ecosystem services and natural resources on which their livelihoods depend;

• national policies which often unintentionally disadvantage poor people and communities by failing to protect their rights and livelihood assets.

These barriers can be overcome through provision of training, support for market and product development, provision of grants or loans through mechanisms and at rates that poor people can access and afford, allocation of secure property rights to poor people and communities, and reform of national policies. It is possible to provide training and support for market and product development through the tourism sector, but removal of other barriers depends on actions by government. Overcoming these barriers is important for poverty alleviation, and also contributes to protection of biodiversity by reducing the pressures that drive poor people to overexploit ecosystem services and natural assets in order to survive.

The programmatic approach of the UNDP/UNEP Poverty-Environment Initiative[4] provides a framework for mainstreaming poverty-environment linkages into national development planning (figure 2), and can also be applied to planning and coordination of sustainable tourism with poverty alleviation and biodiversity conservation, by involving tourism ministries along with environment, protected areas, finance and planning ministries. It illustrates the need for many different stakeholders, and particularly different government ministries, to be involved in formulating plans and programmes for poverty-environment mainstreaming, for implementation of supporting policy measures and for strengthening of institutions and capacity to implement agreed programmes.

The lessons from tourism and poverty alleviation projects are that tourism is better placed than many other sectors in relating to the needs of the poor,[5] but that the commercial and market factors that affect the potential for tourism in any area also need to be taken into account; and that it is also necessary to address wider constraints which keep people in poverty, so that poor people can then benefit from the opportunities offered by tourism. This approach requires careful planning and preparation to ensure that it is focused on sites where conditions exist that maximise the likelihood of success.

---

4   The following paragraphs are based on the UNDP-UNEP Poverty-Environment Initiative's publication *Mainstreaming Poverty-Environment Linkages into Development Planning: A Handbook for Practitioners.*

5   World Tourism Organization (2004), *Tourism and Poverty Alleviation – Recommendations for Action,* UNWTO, Madrid.

Figure 2   Framework for mainstreaming poverty-environment linkages into national development planning

Finding the Entry Points and Making the Case	Mainstreaming Poverty-Environment Linkages into Policy Processes	Meeting the Implementation Challenge
Preliminary assessments Understanding the poverty-environment linkages Understanding the governmental, institutional and political contexts	Collecting country-specific evidence Integrated ecosystem assessment Economic analysis	Including poverty-environment issues in the monitoring system Indicators and data collection
	Influencing poverty processes National (PRSP/MDG) sector and subnational levels	Budgeting and finance Financial support for policy measures
Raising awareness and building partnerships National consensus and commitment	Developing and costing policy measures National, sector and subnational levels	Supporting policy measures National, sector and subnational levels
Strengthening institutions and capacities Needs assessment Working mechanisms	Strengthening institutions and capacities Learning by doing	Strengthening institutions and capacities Mainstreaming as standard practice

Engaging stakeholders and coordinating with the development community
Government, non-governmental and development actors

Source: UNDP/UNEP Poverty-Environment Initiative (2009), *Mainstreaming Poverty-Environment Linkages into Development Planning: A Handbook for Practitioners.*

Chapter 7

Recommendations for Actions on Biodiversity and Tourism by Governments, International Organisations, the Tourism Private Sector and NGOs

As this publication describes, biodiversity is a key asset for tourism, and it is important for the long-term sustainability of tourism to value and protect biodiversity. Protection of biodiversity and the ecosystem services that biodiversity and healthy ecosystems provide, is one of the elements of the agenda for sustainable tourism set out by UNWTO and UNEP.

Addressing tourism **and** biodiversity requires a combined understanding of both tourism and biodiversity, the ways each are managed through various national, local and international institutions, and the interactions between them. In addition, biodiversity-based tourism also is an element of some poverty alleviation programmes: therefore poverty alleviation frameworks also need to be taken into account when addressing relevant aspects of tourism and biodiversity. Tourism, biodiversity protection and poverty alleviation generally operate within different frameworks: the challenge is to bridge these frameworks and the institutions and personnel with responsibilities for them, in order to develop a common approach that maximises benefits for all three areas.

The TEEB study clearly sets out the need to include the value of biodiversity and ecosystem services in all areas of policy and decision-making. Past failures to account for the value of biodiversity and ecosystems have led to overuse resulting in damage to ecosystem services that has major economic downsides, and which is costly and difficult, or in many cases, impossible to replace by technological means. This has been further complicated by a tendency for different branches of government to formulate sectoral policies with little reference to each other. The TEEB emphasises the importance of understanding the Total Economic Value (TEV) of biodiversity and ecosystem services, taking account the multiple uses that are made of these resources; and that this necessitates an integrated approach to policy making and decisions, that brings together all the stakeholders across government in order to formulate and implement common policies.

Recognising the importance of biodiversity for tourism, UNWTO has been actively implementing the CBD Guidelines on Biodiversity and Tourism, which were adopted in 2004, and in 2009 assisted the CBD to produce *Tourism for Nature and Development: A Good Practice Guide*. UNWTO has also been working with various governments and development agencies on tourism and poverty alleviation projects under the Sustainable Tourism – Eliminating Poverty (ST-EP) programme. The lessons from these activities by UNWTO are that the CBD Guidelines provide an effective framework for integrating tourism with biodiversity protection, and for addressing the biodiversity and ecosystem service components of sustainable tourism.

Furthermore, the Tourism Chapter for the Green Economy Report, that is being prepared by UNWTO and UNEP in parallel with this report, identifies "green tourism" models that can reduce negative impacts on the environment while contributing to enhance economic development. The chapter will also address the crucial issue of ensuring that tourism responds effectively to environmental challenges, including biodiversity loss, ecosystems degradation and climate change, through a win-win approach that balances the economic goals of the tourism industry with sustainability criteria and aims. Based on the work that UNWTO has undertaken in these areas, and the framework set out by the TEEB study and the Green Economy Initiative, the recommendations in this section are designed to ensure that tourism is managed and developed in ways that avoid or minimise any damage to biodiversity, that integrated approaches are more widely used to bring together tourism planning with biodiversity management and planning for other uses of natural resources, and that the value of biodiversity for tourism is fully appreciated and taken into account.

The following recommendations apply to UNWTO, governments (national and destination level), the tourism sector, IGOs and NGOs, with implementation varying according to the roles and responsibilities of each of these entities:

1   Promote and implement best practices for avoiding or minimising negative impacts of tourism on biodiversity

The way in which tourism is operated, sited and developed has significant effects on biodiversity. Operational impacts on biodiversity arise from use of natural resources, including energy, water, food and other supplies, the spread of invasive alien species and the effects of physical disturbance and damage caused by tourists on the sites they visit; and tourism facilities need to be carefully sited and developed, since these aspects affect the significance of subsequent operational impacts, and even the most sustainably operated hotel will have major impacts if built in a biodiversity-sensitive area.

There are many examples of best practices that are being applied in the tourism sector, including use of specific technologies, operational methods and standards that result in reduced pressures on biodiversity. Guidance on best practices has been developed by the Tour Operators' Initiative for Sustainable Tourism Development in association with various organizations, for example, covering marine recreation, and tourism in mountain and desert areas.[1] IUCN and the Accor Hotel Group have produced guidelines for hotels on sustainable use of biological resources,[2] including on controlling the spread of invasive alien species. The International Tourism Partnership[3] has produced guidance on best practices in siting and design of tourism facilities. In addition, tourism bodies, NGOs, universities and other institutions have produced guidance on best practices at national or regional level.

Guidance on best practices for avoiding or minimising the impacts of tourism activities on biodiversity needs to be promoted widely to, and implemented by the tourism sector.

It is also recommended that UNWTO compile a directory of guidance on best practices for avoiding or minimising the impacts of tourism activities and development on biodiversity.

2   Integrate biodiversity considerations into national and local sustainable tourism plans, and in planning decisions on tourism development

Biodiversity is a major asset for tourism. It is important that it is protected as a resource for tourism, as well as from the negative impacts that inappropriate or excessive tourism has on biodiversity. To enable better coordination between biodiversity management and tourism, biodiversity considerations, as set out in national biodiversity plans and strategies, need to be taken fully into account in national and local sustainable tourism plans, both by revision of existing tourism plans, and by incorporating biodiversity considerations into preparation of future tourism plans and strategies; and in planning decisions on proposed tourism development.

In addition, the cumulative effects of tourism on biodiversity need to be assessed, and where appropriate, it may be necessary to set limits on tourism development, and/or level and frequency of visitation in some areas, in order to balance tourism with other uses of biodiversity so as to avoid damage to biodiversity through overuse or overdevelopment.

Various practical tools and methods are available and suitable for use in improving coordination between biodiversity management and tourism at national and local levels. These include establishing inter-departmental coordination between the departments with tourism and with biodiversity management responsibilities; Strategic Environmental Assessment (SEA); and Integrated Policy Making for Sustainable Development (IPSD). Various planning methods and approaches are also available to assist with the

---

1   http://www.toinitiative.org/.

2   http://www.iucn.org/about/work/programmes/business/bbp_our_work/tourism/.

3   http://www.tourismpartnership.org/.

integrated management of tourism and biodiversity including the Recreational Opportunity Spectrum and Limits of Acceptable Change.[4]

3   Use the CBD Guidelines on Biodiversity and Tourism Development to assist implementation of the biodiversity and ecosystem service components of sustainable tourism

Protection of biodiversity is one of the elements of sustainable tourism, for example, as set out in the Global Sustainable Tourism Criteria, and in the policy approach and agenda set out in the UNEP/UNWTO publication *Making Tourism More Sustainable*. The GSTC reflect both the CBD Guidelines and the UNWTO Code of Ethics for Tourism, and collectively these provide a firm basis for implementation of sustainable tourism, including biodiversity and ecosystem service components.

UNWTO is actively implementing the CBD Guidelines through its Consulting Unit on Tourism and Biodiversity. The experience gained demonstrates that the CBD Guidelines on Biodiversity and Tourism Development provide an effective framework to assist implementation of the biodiversity and ecosystem service components of sustainable tourism policies and plans, at national, local and site levels, and to build collaboration between those with responsibility for biodiversity management and the tourism sector.

4   Apply the findings of the TEEB to the sustainable management and development of tourism

The TEEB study has highlighted that biodiversity conservation makes economic sense. Failure to protect biodiversity has led to loss of valuable ecosystem services, and the TEEB sets out key policy approaches and management actions that are designed to correct this failure. These are based on assessing the Total Economic Value of biodiversity, along with measures to factor this into policy and decision making in order to correct distortions that have arisen by ignoring the value of biodiversity.

The measures set out in the TEEB include correct pricing of ecosystem services; payments for ecosystem services (PES); reform of subsidies to remove those that damage biodiversity, and to introduce incentives for biodiversity conservation and sustainable development; and using regulation and pricing to establish environmental standards and protect against further losses. The TEEB also highlights the importance of collaboration and partnerships for creating these changes at all levels.

It is also recommended that UNWTO play an important role in implementation of the TEEB by working with other UN organisations, with Tourism Ministries, National Tourism Boards and Destinations and with the tourism private sector, to establish practical ways to apply the findings of the TEEB to the sustainable management and development of tourism.

5   Promote investment in ecological infrastructure that protects and supports tourism

The TEEB emphasises the value of investing in ecological infrastructure – including effective management and expansion of protected areas, and restoration of ecosystem services, for example, by rehabilitating reefs and forested areas. In many cases, investments in ecological infrastructure create opportunities for tourism, and tourism revenues can help contribute to the long-term success of such investments. The potential for governments and the tourism sector to invest in ecological infrastructure that protects and supports tourism needs to be promoted widely to, and implemented by governments and the tourism sector; and also integrated into national sustainable tourism plans and strategies.

4   Secretariat of the Convention on Biological Diversity (2007), *Managing Tourism and Biodiversity, Users' Manual on the CBD Guidelines on Biodiversity and Tourism Development*, Secretariat of the CBD,Montreal.

6   Minimise impacts on biodiversity from adaptation of tourism to climate change

Climate change is affecting biodiversity and economic activities, including tourism. As tourism adapts to climate change it is important to avoid shifting tourism to new and potentially more sensitive areas which would create additional pressures on biodiversity. At the same time, targeted management of biodiversity, such as protection or restoration of coral reefs, coastal ecosystems, wetlands and montane forests, can also assist adaptation and resilience of existing tourism to climate change.

Reduction of carbon emissions remains a priority in the tourism sector, both by using energy more efficiently and by increasing the use of renewable sources of energy, as promoted by the Hotel Energy Solutions project[5]. Alongside this, there is scope also for use of voluntary biodiversity-friendly carbon offset mechanisms with accredited verification procedures for carbon emissions reductions achieved through these mechanisms.

7   Ensure that where projects use tourism as a tool to support biodiversity conservation and/or poverty alleviation, the tourism components have a clear economic base

The success or otherwise of tourism activities and developments depends on market demand from tourists and linkages with other businesses in the tourism value chain. Where tourism is considered as a component in conservation and/or development projects, it is therefore important to take into account the realistic level of market demand; whether there would be sufficient linkages with the tourism value chain, and the probability that the tourism component will be commercially viable and therefore able to make an effective and on-going contribution to biodiversity conservation and poverty alleviation. While tourism can and does make important contributions to biodiversity conservation and poverty alleviation, it can only do so in situations where market demand and linkages with the tourism value chain are sufficient to ensure commercial viability, and is not appropriate in situations where this does not apply.

There is also a need to undertake more extensive monitoring and evaluation of outcomes of projects that include tourism components so as to better understand the effectiveness of these components in relation to tourism and overall project objectives, those factors that contribute to their success, and any problems that have been experienced and how these have been overcome. Findings from such evaluations, also building on the UNWTO and SNV *Manual on Tourism and Poverty Alleviation*[6] as well as experience gained through UNWTO's ST-EP projects, would provide a useful basis for elaboration of guidance for identifying where tourism can be used most effectively as a component of conservation and/or poverty alleviation projects, and on the design and planning of tourism as a component of such projects.

8   Increase knowledge and understanding about the linkages between biodiversity, ecosystem services and tourism

One of the findings of the TEEB is that there is a need to increase knowledge and understanding about the linkages between biodiversity, ecosystem services and the economy. This applies as much to tourism as other sectors. In relation to tourism, there is a need for greater understanding of the contribution of biodiversity and ecosystem services to tourism and destination quality; of the indicators and methodologies that can be applied to assess this, for example, building on the UNWTO publication *Indicators of Sustainable Development for Tourism Destinations: A Guidebook*[7], and to integrate the value of biodiversity into tourism planning and decision-making, and into tourism satellite accounts;

5   www.hotelenergysolutions.net

6   World Tourism Organization and Netherlands Development Organization (2010), *Manual on Tourism and Poverty Alleviation – Practical Steps for Destinations*, UNWTO and SNV, Madrid.

7   World Tourism Organization (2004), *Indicators of Sustainable Development for Tourism Destinations: A Guidebook*, UNWTO, Madrid.

of the pressures and impacts on biodiversity from tourism, and of the relationship between tourism and other uses of biodiversity; of the techniques, technologies and actions that tourism businesses can take for long-term protection of biodiversity; and of ways to raise awareness of tourism businesses and tourists about the importance of biodiversity and its conservation.

9. Promote sustainable tourism products and activities linked to protection of biodiversity

Sustainable tourism products and activities linked to biodiversity conservation and protection of biodiversity assets, help to demonstrate the value of biodiversity for tourism and to generate income that can be invested back into biodiversity and maintenance of ecosystem services. There are many examples of this, and UNWTO has prepared guidance on development of biodiversity-based sustainable tourism products and activities;[8] such products and activities need to be promoted to, and implemented more widely by the tourism sector.

There are also opportunities for UNWTO to collaborate with the Secretariat ot the CBD on promotion and capacity building on tourism concessions in protected areas, to strengthen the ability of protected areas' agencies, particularly in developing countries, to develop partnerships with tourism operators to promote suitable investments that also generate resources for the protected areas, and provide livelihood and business opportunities for indigenous and local communities; and on promotion of biodiversity-friendly indigenous tourism.

10 Involve all relevant stakeholders in evaluating and determining the balance between use of ecosystem services for management and development of sustainable tourism, and other sustainable uses

The TEEB points out that multiple uses are supported by biodiversity and ecosystem services in any area; and that maximising sustainable use should focus on the Total Economic Value taking all uses into account. Maximising the value obtained from a single use, whether this is for tourism or a different use, may well negatively affect other uses, and is unlikely to maximise sustainable use. The TEEB emphasises the need to involve all relevant stakeholders in identification of the various different uses made of biodiversity and ecosystem services associated with any area, and in determination of the value of those services, and the appropriate balance between different uses of that area. This is consistent with the aims of sustainable tourism in particular its aims relating to social equity, local control, community wellbeing, and biological diversity, and with Articles 3 and 5 of the *Global Code of Ethics for Tourism*.

---

8   World Tourism Organization, (2010), *Practical Guide for the Development of Biodiversity-based Tourism Products*, UNWTO, Madrid.

Chapter 8

Conclusion

Protecting biodiversity is an issue of critical national and international importance. The TEEB study demonstrates the economic value of biodiversity and the ecosystem services it provides; and that this needs to be fully taken into account in planning and decision-making by all levels of government, the private sector and other stakeholders. Combined with this, the 2010 and post-2010 biodiversity goals established under the CBD provide a strategy for halting and reversing biodiversity loss.

The evidence presented in this report shows the high value of biodiversity for tourism. Biodiversity is a vital component of the environmental quality and attraction of destinations for tourists, and needs to be protected for the long-term success of tourism. Effective application of land use planning and development controls in destinations to influence new and existing tourism activities and to prevent potentially harmful developments, are particularly important for the success of tourism and for achieving protection of biodiversity and ecosystem services, in line with the 2010 and post-2010 biodiversity goals, and the recommendations of the TEEB.

Many countries and destinations already have strategies and policies for tourism and for biodiversity. However, the integration between them may often need to be strengthened: this can be done as part of the process of their revision and review, drawing on the recommendations in this report. Where these strategies and policies are being developed for the first time, this integration can be built in from the outset. Likewise, the private sector and other stakeholders are encouraged to take action to minimise, and where possible avoid, adverse impacts from tourism on biodiversity.

With the international recognition of the need to halt and reverse biodiversity loss, the time is right for all those involved in tourism – governments, at national, local and destination levels, the private sector and other stakeholders – to implement and strengthen policies and actions to help achieve this goal.

List of Tables, Boxes and Figures

Tables

Table 1   Relationship between Processes for Implementation of
           CBD Guidelines and Sustainable Tourism 21

Table 2   Available solutions for better stewardship of natural capital proposed by the TEEB study 29

Boxes

Box 1   Ecosystem services 2

Box 2   UNWTO Consulting Unit on Tourism and Biodiversity 4

Box 3   Multiple uses of biodiversity 11

Box 4   Some examples of the value of parks, protected areas and wildlife for tourism 15

Box 5   Development of the *CBD Guidelines on Biodiversity and Tourism Development* 20

Box 6   The Economics of Ecosystems and Biodiversity – Key conclusions 28

Box 7   Tourism and ecosystem services – Economic flows using protected areas as
          an example of an ecosystem service 31

Box 8   Sustainable tourism and biodiversity conservation in Pangandaran, Indonesia 34

Box 9   Policy processes for sustainable tourism in Mexico, Namibia and Malta 35

Box 10   Extracts from the *Global Code of Ethics for Tourism* addressing sustainable development,
          environmental protection and benefits for host countries and communities 38

Box 11   ST-EP Project – Cambodia: Mekong Discovery Trail and Tourism Development Master Plan
          for Kratie Town 41

Figures

Figure 1   Examples of poverty-environment linkages 40

Figure 2   Framework for mainstreaming poverty-environment linkages into national
           development planning 43

Annex 1

Typology of ecosystem services

The following typology of ecosystem services is used in the TEEB, along with the supporting services identified in the MA:

Main service-types

Provisioning services
• Food (e.g. fish, game, fruit)
• Water (e.g. for drinking, irrigation, cooling)
• Raw materials (e.g. fiber, timber, fuel wood, fodder, fertilizer)
• Genetic resources (e.g. for crop improvement and medicinal purposes)
• Medicinal resources (e.g. biochemical products, models and test organisms)
• Ornamental resources (e.g. artisan work, decorative plants, pet animals, fashion)

Regulating services
• Air quality regulation (e.g. capturing (fine) dust, chemicals, etc.)
• Climate regulation (incl. C-sequestration, influence of vegetation on rainfall, etc.)
• Moderation of extreme events (e.g. storm protection and flood prevention)
• Regulation of water flows (e.g. natural drainage, irrigation and drought prevention)
• Waste treatment (especially water purification)
• Erosion prevention
• Maintenance of soil fertility (incl. soil formation)
• Pollination
• Biological control (e.g. seed dispersal, pest and disease control)

Habitat services
• Maintenance of life cycles of migratory species (incl. nursery service)
• Maintenance of genetic diversity (especially gene pool protection)

Cultural services
• Aesthetic information
• Opportunities for recreation and tourism
• Inspiration for culture, art and design
• Spiritual experience
• Information for cognitive development

Supporting services (from millennium ecosystem assessment, 2005)
• Nutrient cycling (Role ecosystems play in the flow and recycling of nutrients (e.g., nitrogen, sulphur, phosphorus, carbon) through processes such as decomposition and/or absorption)
• Primary production (Formation of biological material by plants through photosynthesis and nutrient assimilation)
• Water cycling (Flow of water through ecosystems)

From: *The Economics of Ecosystems and Biodiversity: The Ecological and Economic Foundations* (TEEB D0), Chapter 1 and Appendix 2 [Source: based on/adapted mainly from Costanza et al. (1997), De Groot et al. (2002), MA (2005a), Daily et al. (2008); see TEEB, Appendix 2 for details.], and Millennium Ecosystem Assessment, 2005 (Supporting Services).

Impacts of Tourism on the Environment and Biodiversity

Impacts of tourism in relation to the environment and biological diversity may include:

a) Use of land and resources for accommodation, tourism facilities and other infrastructure provision, including road networks, airports and seaports

b) Extraction and use of building materials (e.g., use of sand from beaches, reef limestone and wood)

c) Damage to or destruction of ecosystems and habitats, including deforestation, draining of wetlands, and intensified or unsustainable use of land

d) Increased risk of erosion

e) Disturbance of wild species, disrupting normal behaviour and potentially affecting mortality and reproductive success

f) Alterations to habitats and ecosystems

g) Increased risk of fires

h) Unsustainable consumption of flora and fauna by tourists (e.g., through picking of plants; or purchase of souvenirs manufactured from wildlife, in particular such endangered species as corals and turtle shells; or through unregulated hunting, shooting and fishing)

i) Increased risk of introduction of alien species

j) Intensive water demand from tourism

k) Extraction of groundwater

l) Deterioration in water quality (freshwater, coastal waters) and sewage pollution

m) Eutrophication of aquatic habitats

n) Introduction of pathogens

o) Generation, handling and disposal of sewage and waste-water

p) Chemical wastes, toxic substances and pollutants

q) Solid waste (garbage or rubbish)

r) Contamination of land, freshwater and seawater resources

s) Pollution and production of greenhouse gases, resulting from travel by air, road, rail, or sea, at local, national and global levels

t) Noise

© 2010 World Tourism Organization – ISBN 978-92-844-1371-3

Socio-economic and cultural impacts related to tourism may include:

a)   Influx of people and social degradation (e.g. local prostitution, drug abuse, etc.)

b)   Impacts on children and youth

c)   Vulnerability to the changes in the flow of tourist arrivals which may result in sudden loss of income and jobs in times of downturn

d)   Impacts on indigenous and local communities and cultural values

e)   Impacts on health and the integrity of local cultural systems

f)   Intergenerational conflicts and changed gender relationships

g)   Erosion of traditional practices and lifestyles

h)   Loss of access by indigenous and local communities to their land and resources as well as sacred sites, which are integral to the maintenance of traditional knowledge systems and traditional lifestyles

Potential benefits of tourism may include:

a)   Revenue creation for the maintenance of natural resources of the area

b)   Contributions to economic and social development, for example:

   i)   Funding the development of infrastructure and services

   ii)   Providing jobs

   iii)   Providing funds for development or maintenance of sustainable practices

   iv)   Providing alternative and supplementary ways for communities to receive revenue from biological diversity

   v)   Generating incomes

   vi)   Education and empowerment

   vii) An entry product that can have direct benefits for developing other related products at the site and regionally

   viii) Tourist satisfaction and experience gained at tourist destination

   ix)   Providing alternative and supplementary ways for communities to receive revenue from biological diversity

   x)   Generating incomes

   xi)   Education and empowerment

   xii) An entry product that can have direct benefits for developing other related products at the site and regionally

   xiii) Tourist satisfaction and experience gained at tourist destination

Source: Articles 41, 42 and 43 of the Secretariat of the Convention on Biological Diversity (2004), *Guidelines on Biodiversity and Tourism Development* – International guidelines for activities related to sustainable tourism development in vulnerable terrestrial, marine and coastal ecosystems and habitats of major importance for biological diversity and protected areas, including fragile riparian and mountain ecosystems, Secretariat of the CBD, Montreal.

The 12 Aims for Sustainable Tourism

The 12 aims for an agenda for sustainable tourism are:

1)	Economic Viability
	To ensure the viability and competitiveness of tourism destinations and enterprises, so that they are able to continue to prosper and deliver benefits in the long term.
2)	Local Prosperity
	To maximize the contribution of tourism to the economic prosperity of the host destination, including the proportion of visitor spending that is retained locally.
3)	Employment Quality
	To strengthen the number and quality of local jobs created and supported by tourism, including the level of pay, conditions of service and availability to all without discrimination by gender, race, disability or in other ways.
4)	Social Equity
	To seek a widespread and fair distribution of economic and social benefits from tourism throughout the recipient community, including improving opportunities, income and services available to the poor.
5)	Visitor Fulfillment
	To provide a safe, satisfying and fulfilling experience for visitors, available to all without discrimination by gender, race, disability or in other ways.
6)	Local Control
	To engage and empower local communities in planning and decision making about the management and future development of tourism in their area, in consultation with other stakeholders.
7)	Community Wellbeing
	To maintain and strengthen the quality of life in local communities, including social structures and access to resources, amenities and life support systems, avoiding any form of social degradation or exploitation.
8)	Cultural Richness
	To respect and enhance the historic heritage, authentic culture, traditions and distinctiveness of host communities.
9)	Physical Integrity
	To maintain and enhance the quality of landscapes, both urban and rural, and avoid the physical and visual degradation of the environment.
10)	Biological Diversity
	To support the conservation of natural areas, habitats and wildlife, and minimize damage to them.
11)	Resource Efficiency
	To minimize the use of scarce and non-renewable resources in the development and operation of tourism facilities and services.
12)	Environmental Purity
	To minimize the pollution of air, water and land and the generation of waste by tourism enterprises and visitors.

Source: UNEP and UNWTO (2005), *Making Tourism More Sustainable – A Guide for Policy Makers.*

Annex 4

ST-EP Projects
Associated with Biodiversity-based Tourism

Country/Region	Full Title	Principal Funding Source
Africa		
Benin	Promotion and Development of Sustainable Tourism in the Buffer Zone of Park W	Italian Government
Burkina Faso	Development of Community-based Tourism in the Buffer Zone of Park W	Italian Government
Cameroon	Development of a Network for Promotion and Capacity Building for Running Bird Watching Tours	SNV
Ethiopia	Ecotourism Development in Bale Mountains National Park	SNV
Ghana	West Coast Tourism Destination Area Development	Italian Government
Guinea	Ecotourism Development in Sangareah in the Dubreka Region	ST-EP Foundation
Kenya	The Kitengela Footbridge Project	ST-EP Foundation
	Business Case for Wildlife Conservation in Kasigau Community	ST-EP Foundation
	Enhancement of Local Employment in Amboseli Tourism Destination through the Creation of a Pioneer Vocational Tourism Training School	IUCN Netherlands
Madagascar	Development of Community-based Ecotourism in the Anjozorobe-Angavo Protected Area	ST-EP Foundation
Mali	Strengthening the Capacities of Tourism Stakeholders at Douentza and d'Hombori within the Framework of Ecotourism Development and Promotion of the Elephants of Gourma	ST-EP Foundation
	Expanding Ecotourism Activities: Agricultural Supply to Hotels in Sangha	Italian Government
	Supporting Female Entrepreneurs through the Strengthening of Handicrafts and Agrobusiness in the Region of Mopti	AECID
	Expanding Ecotourism Activities: Ecotourism Promotion in Siby	Italian Government
	Expanding Ecotourism Activities: Guides Training in Djenné, Sangha and Siby	
	Expanding Ecotourism Activities: Guides Training in Mopti	
Mozambique	Community-based Lodges Training Programme	ST-EP Foundation Flemish Government
Niger	Valorisation of Tourism in the Buffer Zone of Park W by the Establishment of Micro-Enterprises	Italian Government
Rwanda	Congo-Nile Trails	SNV ST-EP Foundation UNWTO

Country/Region	Full Title	Principal Funding Source
Africa		
United Republic of Tanzania	Pangani – Saadani Coastal Protection	ST-EP Foundation
	Uluguru Mountains Ecotourism Project	ST-EP Foundation IUCN Netherlands
Latin America		
Bolivia	Strengthening Rural Community-based Tourism and Commercial Management to Consolidate the Inca Trail (Qhapac-Ñan Project)	SNV ST-EP Foundation UNWTO
Ecuador	Sustainable Tourism in Protected Areas	SNV
	Fostering Rural Community-based Tourism and Inclusive Business within the Framework of Effective Destination Management along the Inca Trail (Qhapac-Ñan Project)	SNV ST-EP Foundation UNWTO
	Fostering Sustainable Tourism through the Development of Inclusive Business in Galapagos Islands	
Peru	Sustainable Tourism and Birdwatching at Luichupucro	ST-EP Foundation
	Strengthening Rural Community-based Tourism in Aypate within the Framework of Effective Destination Management along the Inca Trail (Quapac-Ñan Project)	SNV ST-EP Foundation UNWTO
	Strengthening Rural Community-based Tourism in Puno within the Framework of Effective Destination Management along the Inca Trail (Qhapac-Ñan Project)	
Asia		
Cambodia	Mekong Discovery Trail and Tourism Development Master Plan for Kratie Town	SNV
	Mekong Discovery Trail	SNV ST-EP Foundation UNWTO
Lao People's Democratic Republic	Canopy Walkway and Zip Line: a new tourist attraction at Dong Hua Sao National Park	ST-EP Foundation IUCN Netherlands
	Upgrading Local Facilities to Promote Community-based Elephant Tourism and Nature Conservation in the Hongsa District	
	Capacity Building in Conservation Planning and Management in Viengxay District	SNV
Nepal	Great Himalaya Trail Development in West Nepal: Linking Formal and Informal Enterprises to Tourism Markets to Reduce Poverty	SNV ST-EP Foundation UNWTO
Vietnam	Promoting Pro-Poor Sustainable Tourism for Livelihood Improvement and Biodiversity Conservation in Coastal Tam Giang Lagoon, Thua Thien Hue Province	ST-EP Foundation IUCN Netherlands

Annex 5

ST-EP Mechanisms and Principles for Pursuing Poverty Alleviation Through Tourism

Seven ST-EP Mechanisms

1. Employment of the poor in tourism enterprises

2. Supply of goods and services to tourism enterprises by the poor or by enterprises employing the poor

3. Direct sales of goods and services to visitors by the poor (informal economy)

4. Establishment and running of tourism enterprises by the poor – e.g. micro, small and medium sized enterprises (MSMEs), or community based enterprises (formal economy)

5. Tax or levy on tourism income or profits with proceeds benefiting the poor

6. Voluntary giving/support by tourism enterprises and tourists

7. Investment in infrastructure stimulated by tourism also benefiting the poor in the locality, directly or through support to other sectors

Ten Principles for pursuing poverty alleviation through tourism

1. All aspects and types of tourism can and should be concerned about poverty alleviation

2. All governments should include poverty alleviation as a key aim of tourism development and consider tourism as a possible tool for alleviating poverty

3. The competitiveness and economic success of tourism businesses and destinations is critical to poverty alleviation – without this the poor cannot benefit

4. All tourism businesses should be concerned about the impact of their activities on local communities and seek to benefit the poor through their actions

5. Tourism destinations should be managed with poverty alleviation as a central aim that is built into strategies and action plans

6. A sound understanding of how tourism functions in destinations is required, including how tourism income is distributed and who benefits from this

7. Planning and development of tourism in destinations should involve a wide range of interests, including participation and representation from poor communities

8. All potential impacts of tourism on the livelihood of local communities should be considered, including current and future local and global impacts on natural and cultural resources

9. Attention must be paid to the viability of all projects involving the poor, ensuring access to markets and maximizing opportunities for beneficial links with established enterprises

10. Impacts of tourism on poverty alleviation should be effectively monitored

Source: UNWTO and SNV (2010), *Manual on Tourism and Poverty Alleviation – Practical Steps for Destinations.*

Further Reading

International Tourism Partnership (2010), *Sustainable Hotel Siting, Design and Construction* (Online), available: http://www.tourismpartnership.org/Publications/Publications.html

IUCN (2008), *Biodiversity: My hotel in Action – A guide to Sustainable Use of Biological Resources* (Online), available: http://www.iucn.org/about/work/programmes/business/bbp_our_work/tourism/

Millennium Ecosystem Assessment (2005), *Ecosystems and Human Well-being: Synthesis* (Online), available: http://www.millenniumassessment.org/

Secretariat of the Convention on Biological Diversity (2004), *Guidelines on Biodiversity and Tourism Development* (Online), available: http://www.cbd.int/tourism/guidelines.shtml

Secretariat of the Convention on Biological Diversity (2007), *Users' Manual on the CBD Guidelines on Biodiversity and Tourism Development* (Online), available: http://tourism.cbd.int/documents/cbdtourismmanual.pdf

Secretariat of the Convention on Biological Diversity (2008), *Protected Areas in Today's World: Their Values and Benefits for the Welfare of the Planet,* Technical Series no. 36 (Online), available: http://www.cbd.int/

Secretariat of the Convention on Biological Diversity (2008), *The Value of Nature: Ecological, Economic, Cultural and Social Benefits of Protected Areas* (Online), available: http://www.cbd.int/

Secretariat of the Convention on Biological Diversity (2010), *Global Biodiversity Outlook 3* (Online), available: http://gbo3.cbd.int/

The Economics of Ecosystems and Biodiversity (TEEB) (2009), *The Economics of Ecosystems and Biodiversity for National and International Policy Makers – Summary: Responding to the Value of Nature* (Online), available: http://teebweb.org/

The Economics of Ecosystems and Biodiversity (TEEB) (2010), *The Economics of Ecosystems and Biodiversity Report for Business* (Online), available: http://teebweb.org/

Tour Operators' Initiative (2004), *Supply Chain Engagement for Tour Operators: Three steps toward sustainability* (Online), available: http://www.toinitiative.org/

Tour Operators' Initiative (2006), *Tourism and Deserts: A Practical Guide to Managing the Social and Environmental Impacts in the Desert Recreation Sector* (with self-evaluation checklist) available in English, French and Arabic (Online), available: http://www.toinitiative.org/

Tour Operators' Initiative (2007), *Tourism and Mountains: A Practical Guide to Managing the Environmental and Social Impacts of Mountain Tours* (with self-evaluation checklist) available in English, Spanish and French (Online), available: http://www.toinitiative.org/

Tour Operators' Initiative, *A Practical Guide to Good Practice: Managing Environmental Impacts in the Marine Recreation Sector* (with self-evaluation checklist), available in English, Spanish and French (Online), available: http://www.toinitiative.org/

Tourism Sustainability Council (2010), *Global Sustainable Tourism Criteria* (Online), available: http://www.sustainabletourismcriteria.org/

UN's Green Economy Initiative (Online), available: http://www.unep.org/greeneconomy/

UNDP/UNEP Poverty-Environment Initiative (2009), *Mainstreaming Poverty-Environment Linkages into Development Planning: A Handbook for Practitioners* (Online), available: http://www.unpei.org/

© 2010 **World Tourism Organization – ISBN** 978-92-844-1371-3

United Nations Environment Programme (2005), *Forging Links between Protected Areas and the Tourism Sector: How Tourism can Benefit Conservation,* UNEP, Paris (Online), available: http://www.unep.fr/scp/tourism/

United Nations Environment Programme (2010), *Are You a Green Leader? Business and Biodiversity: Making the Case for a Lasting Solution* (Online), available: http://www.unep-wcmc.org/resources/publications/AreYouAGreenLeader.pdf

United Nations Environment Programme – Secretariat of the Convention on Migratory Species (2004) *Wildlife Watching and Tourism: A Study on the Benefits and Risks of a Fast Growing Tourism Activity and Its Impacts on Species* (Online), available: http://www.cms.int/publications/pdf/CMS_WildlifeWatching.pdf

United Nations Environment Programme and Conservation International (2003), *Tourism and Biodiversity – Mapping Tourism's Global Footprint* (Online), available: http://www.unep.fr/scp/tourism/

United Nations Environment Programme and World Tourism Organization (2005) *Making Tourism More Sustainable – A Guide for Policy Makers,* available in English, Spanish and French (Online), available: http://www.unep.fr/scp/publications/

World Tourism Organization (2004), *Global Code of Ethics for Tourism,* UNWTO, Madrid.

World Tourism Organization (2004), *Indicators of Sustainable Development for Tourism Destinations – A Guidebook,* UNWTO, Madrid.

World Tourism Organization (2004), *Tourism and Poverty Alleviation – Recommendations for Action,* UNWTO, Madrid.

World Tourism Organization (2010), *Practical Guide for the Development of Biodiversity-based Tourism Products,* UNWTO, Madrid.

World Tourism Organization and SNV (2010) *Manual on Tourism and Poverty Alleviation – Practical Steps for Destinations,* UNWTO, Madrid.